Tasks in a Pedagogical Context

Multilingual Matters

Please contact us for the latest book information:
Multilingual Matters Ltd,
Frankfurt Lodge, Clevedon Hall, Victoria Road,
Clevedon, Avon BS21 7SJ, England

MULTILINGUAL MATTERS 94
Series Editor: Derrick Sharp

TASKS IN A PEDAGOGICAL CONTEXT
Integrating Theory and Practice

Edited by

Graham Crookes and Susan M. Gass

MULTILINGUAL MATTERS LTD
Clevedon • Philadelphia • Adelaide

Library of Congress Cataloging in Publication Data

Tasks in a Pedagogical Context: Integrating Theory and Practice/
Edited by Graham Crookes and Susan M. Gass
p. cm. (Multilingual Matters: 94)
Includes bibliographical references and index.
1. Language and languages–Study and teaching. 2. Curriculum planning.
3. Task analysis in education. I. Crookes, Graham. II. Gass, Susan M.
III. Series: Multilingual Matters (Series): 94.
P53.295.T37   1993
418′.007–dc20

British Library Cataloguing in Publication Data

A CIP catalogue record for this book is available from the British Library.

ISBN 1-85359-187-4 (hbk)
ISBN 1-85359-186-6 (pbk)

Multilingual Matters Ltd

UK: Frankfurt Lodge, Clevedon Hall, Victoria Road, Clevedon, Avon BS21 7SJ.
USA: 1900 Frost Road, Suite 101, Bristol, PA 19007, USA.
Australia: P.O. Box 6025, 83 Gilles Street, Adelaide, SA 5000, Australia.

Typeset by Wayside Books, Clevedon.
Printed and bound in Great Britain by the Longdunn Press, Bristol.

Contents

Preface

This book stems from a long-standing interest on the part of both of the editors in the notion of tasks. We were both concerned with the extent to which tasks are an important aspect of the teaching/learning process. However, we each approach the topic from a different orientation — Graham Crookes' major interest has been in the pedagogical domain, whereas Susan Gass has been more focused on issues relating to learning. Because we both felt that tasks were of importance from both perspectives and because there was no book which unified these perspectives, we decided to undertake this project.

The task of putting this book together has been truly a global affair. Discussions took place at TESOL, San Francisco, TESOL, San Antonio, TESOL, Chicago, in Michigan and in Hawai'i. We were helped along the way by numerous friends and colleagues, including Josh Ard, Michael Long, Carolyn Madden, Litsa Varonis and John Swales. We are grateful to them for their input and wisdom. We also appreciate the work and effort which our contributors have put into the writing of their individual chapters. Their promptness in responding to our queries, criticisms and suggestions made our task easier.

Introduction

GRAHAM CROOKES
University of Hawai'i
SUSAN GASS
Michigan State University

This book, and its companion volume, *Tasks in Language Learning: Integrating Theory and Practice,* are centrally concerned with the concept of task, as it has developed in the contexts of language learning as well as curriculum and syllabus design.

As is by now well known, the term 'task', used in one sense or another, began to come into deliberate use in applied linguistics around the beginning of the 1980s. We see it as having two major foci — first, as an aspect of the research methodology used in studies of second language acquisition (SLA) from the beginning of the 1980s, and second, as a concept used in second language curriculum design from the middle of the 1980s.

In the SLA literature, the focus on tasks had as its precursor work on conversational analysis of second language speakers. Early work in SLA focused on learners using conversation as a forum for practice of what had been presented in a classroom situation. This view changed in the mid 1970s with work by Wagner-Gough & Hatch (1975). They argued that conversation did not serve the function of mere practice of forms, structures, etc., but was the locus of the development of syntax. As Ellis (1984: 95) states,

> interaction contributes to development because it is the means by which the learner is able to crack the code. This takes place when the learner can infer what is said even though the message contains linguistic items that are not yet part of his competence and when the learner can use the discourse to help him/her modify or supplement the linguistic knowledge already used in production.

Central to these discussions is Long's (1980) distinction between modified input (the language addressed to a non-native speaker [NNS]) and modified interaction. Modified interaction refers to the modification and restructuring of conversational form by all conversational participants, through such means as comprehension checks and clarification requests. These features are claimed to have the effect of increasing the possibilities of mutual intelligibility and of expanding the possibilities which NNSs otherwise have of expressing meaning. Thus, negotiation of the sort prevalent in NNS discourse provides the learner with (1) the opportunity to hear language which may be useful for later integration into her language-learner system, and (2) the possibility of expressing concepts which are beyond her linguistic capacity.

A second argument generally made in favor of the positive function of negotiation stems from work done by Stevick (1976, 1980), who claims that successful communication is dependent on attentiveness and involvement in the discourse by all participants and that it is involvement which facilitates acquisition in that it 'charges' the input, allowing it to 'penetrate'. Much recent work has focused on the concept of attention. Within this framework it is claimed that without conscious attention (Schmidt, 1990) acquisition cannot take place. Gass (1988) has similarly argued that in order for input to become useful to a learner in eventual restructuring of her grammar, it must first be 'noticed'. What negotiation then does is focus a learner's attention on that part of her utterance which has not been successful. That is, it gives an indication that something in the conversation has gone awry and therefore that there are changes which need to be made, although it does not tell learners what changes need to be made. Thus, negotiation can be viewed as a trigger for acquisition. It is one of many possible ways of initiating the long process of modification of one's second language grammar.

With this emphasis on what learners do with language and on what learners learn from it came a focus on how different tasks influence the kind of language which learners produced. Early work focused on different forms used in different tasks (Tarone, 1979). More recent work, however, has had as its primary goal the discovery of interactional features present in different types of discourse and different task types. One of the most important concepts brought to the literature was the distinction between a one-way and a two-way task (Long, 1981) (see chapter by Plough & Gass, fn. 2) and further developed by Duff (1986) in her study of convergent and divergent tasks. The question raised in this work is: what is the relationship between kinds of tasks and the language output? An indirect, but nonetheless central concern in this research tradition is: how does language output relate to acquisition? The chapters in this book, and those in the accompanying volume, further our knowledge in this direction by investigating both of these questions.

This Volume

The chapters in this book deal explicitly with the use of tasks as a pedagogical tool. As the empirical and conceptual literature on task as an element of syllabus design, materials development, and classroom instruction continues to grow, we see little likelihood that those who use this term will agree on what precisely it is they mean by it. One difference in particular should be pointed out here, however. Some writers on this topic follow Breen (e.g. 1984) in considering anything done in the classroom a 'task' — others take a line similar to Long, in restricting the term to describing a section of classroom practice which involves second language learners in carrying out language-based interactions which relate to something they might have to do, using the second language, in the world outside the classroom. We have not in either of these volumes attempted to restrict our contributors to either of the above usages, but have attempted to encourage authors to be clear about their position. It would repay readers to clarify in their own minds how they, too, wish to understand the term.

Despite some minor terminological slippage, all of the authors in this collection are obviously of the opinion that the term is useful, and that work on second language classrooms, syllabus design, and materials development can benefit from a task-oriented perspective. They find, that is to say, that 'task' is a productive analytic unit for looking at classrooms, and a productive unit with which to construct syllabi and materials. Though nearly all contributors use ESL as the basic exemplar, there is nothing in the discussions which would not apply to the teaching of second or foreign languages other than English — indeed, we believe that what is presented in both of these volumes is applicable to the learning and teaching of other second/ foreign languages.

In the initial chapter Long & Crookes provide a background review of major syllabus types that have been used in second language syllabus development. Having looked at the strengths and weaknesses of both the most common syllabus types, such as structural and notional–functional, as well as less-often discussed types such as topical and situational, they attempt to show that though comparatively untried, task-based syllabi in general, and task-based language teaching in particular, are likely to have most to offer the second language teacher and learner, on both empirical and conceptual grounds.

Nunan (in Chapter 2) probes in much more detail than most investigators have hitherto done the various elements that could be argued to make up or be closely associated with the classroom task. His discussion should be particularly useful, we think, to those who wish to design class-room materials that reflect as far as possible what we currently know about SLA, and which, unlike most commercially available materials, are of a principled nature.

The discussion is further developed in Chapter 3 by Kumaravadivelu, who takes issue to some extent with terminological and componential analyses presented in the task-oriented literature thus far. He explores the ambiguity inherent in work on tasks and attempts a definition with regard to three broadly conceived language teaching approaches: (1) language centered, (2) learner centered, and (3) learning centered. Kumaravadivelu's chapter includes a consideration of ways in which teachers can be guided into analyz-ing and selecting tasks for the classroom.

Moving to more empirical work, the chapter by Berwick (Chapter 4) provides a detailed, in-depth analysis of the sort of language which is pro-duced when tasks which differ on certain design features are presented to similar groups of learners. This line of work, empirical investigations of task design, was predicated in the work of Long (1980), and has been a consistent feature throughout task research. For many, studies of this sort are parti-cularly valuable in as much as their long-term implications include the development of a materials design program which is empirically based and directly linked with general SLA research.

Also in this line is the chapter by Samuda & Rounds (Chapter 5). They investigate in a focused way one of the handful of experimental tasks which are used in both SLA research and in work on syllabus design — the 'spot the difference' task. Their research departs from previous work in that they treat the 'spot the difference' task not as a single phenomenon, but as a task which can be characterized as being comprised of different types of stimuli. In their research they find that there are different linguistic outcomes based on the varying linguistic input stimuli. These results are taken as the basis for suggesting ways in which task types may be matched to different student needs.

For logistical reasons, much of the work on tasks has been done under experimental conditions. Yet of course, for reasons of validity, it is neces-sary to see how research on tasks translates to the classroom, and it is also of interest to see how the classroom itself functions in terms of 'task'. One of the arguments for the use of this concept is that several lines of main-stream educational research (e.g. Doyle, 1986; Zahorik, 1975) have indi-cated that the term is meaningful in terms of how teachers and students see the classroom and how teachers plan instruction. So in this context, Murphy in Chapter 6 allows us to demonstrate that important classroom links are being developed in this respect. It also allows a connection to be made to the process syllabus work of Breen (e.g. 1984) and Candlin (e.g. 1984) who stress the role of the learner in syllabus design, and Murphy here presents some straightforward considerations of the way this can happen when students and teacher together make use of the analytic term 'task', a term which is immediately accessible to them.

Tasks and Language Learning: Integrating Theory and Practice

In the accompanying volume, *Tasks in Language Learning: Integrating Theory and Practice,* the focus is on tasks as they are used for research in second language learning. In the first chapter in that book Pica, Kanagy & Falodun taxonomize communication task types, focusing on issues of classroom pedagogy and learning theory. The basis for their taxonomy is *goal* and *activity.* Concepts such as information flow, optimal versus required information requests, collaboration versus independence of participants, and task goals are central to their taxonomy. Their chapter is rich in content not only for the thoroughness of the communication task typology which they present, but also because they take the next important step of linking the different tasks to learner production and learning.

The second chapter focuses on the interlocutor. Specifically, Plough & Gass investigate the extent to which the task participants' familiarity with each other and with the task type affects the linguistic outcome. Through two experiments, they show that both types of familiarity have an effect on production, but that there may be large individual differences which ultimately determine the language which learners produce. As with the Pica, Kanagy & Falodun chapter, Plough & Gass discuss the relationship between the kinds of interactional features present in non-native speaker discourse and acquisition outcomes.

Duff's chapter differs from others in that her data come not from highly structured experimental or classroom-type tasks, but were gathered in a 'naturalistic' setting from a Cambodian immigrant to Canada. The focus of investigation in this study was the lexicon (in particular, lexical variety) and syntax (nominal reference and negotiation). The task types were categorized in terms of interactional direction, source of the prompt and content, both in terms of the nature of the content and the extent to which there was shared information about the content. The results of Duff's study, while pointing to some differences in task, also point to the need to have well-specified differences in order to determine the effect of task on language production.

The chapter by Shortreed follows the tradition set out in the non-native speaker foreigner talk and interaction literature. His concern is with the effect of task complexity and learner proficiency on variables relating to linguistic reduction, and communication and repair strategies on the part of native speakers. His database differs from the typical one in that his non-native speakers are learners of Japanese. The findings both support and refute previous research in this area. As we move to a better understanding of task types and task differences, Shortreed's contribution is significant in that he attempts to reconcile what appear to be conflicting results.

The final chapter bridges the gap between learning outcomes and syllabus design and thus, points the way to the topic of this book. Loschky & Bley-Vroman argue that despite the general orientation of the task line in materials and syllabus development to a communicative approach and away from a structural emphasis, there is nevertheless a role for tasks in structurally oriented second language learning and teaching (though not necessarily within structural syllabi). Specifically, they argue that tasks can offer an opportunity for second language learners to be exposed to and learn from their practice of language which is fairly constrained with regards to the syntactic features it manifests.

Conclusions

We believe that these two collections show the potential strengths of this domain of second language research. Naturally, there are weaknesses, too, and we do not wish to let them go unacknowledged. In particular, bringing syllabus design considerations, which have tended to have a strong 'rational' (i.e. non-empirical) bent over the years to closer quarters with real-life investigations of how teachers and learners actually operate, is particularly difficult. The problem, of course, is that so many factors intervene between syllabus type and learning. Even when we consider materials formats, the problems caused for investigators by the factors which stand between learner and textbook are considerable. Nevertheless, they must be addressed by researchers, and we hope that the discussions presented here will be useful.

In addition, as second language teachers as well as researchers, we find the concept of 'task' extremely helpful in conceptualizing what we do. We hope, therefore, that fellow teachers who look over these pages will find that the concepts presented here stimulate their professional curiosity. There is an enormous need for those whose professional career has allowed them to concentrate heavily on investigation to ensure that their ideas are validated by practitioners. At the same time, the accumulation of evidence concerning second language learning will be too slow unless all teachers become more and more involved. That is to say, we feel we can close this introduction with the phrase, hallowed by tradition, 'further research is needed' — but we want to emphasize that it needs to be done and can be done by *all* of us. We hope that these two books will provide the basis for research on tasks from both a learning and a pedagogical perspective.

References

BREEN, M. 1984, Process syllabuses for the language classroom. *ELT Documents* 118, 47–60.

CANDLIN, C. 1984, Syllabus design as a critical process. *ELT Documents* 118, 29–46.

DOYLE, W. 1986, Academic tasks in classrooms. In M. HAMMERSLEY (ed.) *Case Studies in Classroom Research*. Milton Keynes: Open University Press.

DUFF, P. 1986, Another look at interlanguage talk: Taking task to task. In R. DAY (ed.) *Talking to Learn: Conversation in Second Language Acquisition*. Rowley, MA: Newbury House.

ELLIS, R. 1984, *Classroom Second Language Development: A Study of Classroom Interaction and Language Acquisition*. Oxford: Pergamon Press.

GASS, S. 1988, Integrating research areas: A framework for second language studies. *Applied Linguistics* 9, 198–217.

LONG, M. H. 1980, Input, interaction and second language acquisition. Unpublished Ph.D. dissertation, UCLA.

—— 1981, Input, interaction and second language acquisition. In H. WINITZ (ed.) *Native Language and Foreign Language Acquisition*. Annals of the New York Academy of Sciences 379, 259–78.

SCHMIDT, R. 1990, The role of consciousness in second language learning. *Applied Linguistics* 11, 219–58.

STEVICK, E. 1976, *Memory, Meaning and Method*. Rowley, MA: Newbury House.

—— 1980, *Teaching Languages: A Way and Ways*. Rowley, MA: Newbury House.

TARONE, E. 1979, Interlanguage as chameleon. *Language Learning* 29, 181–91.

WAGNER-GOUGH, J. and HATCH, E. 1975, The importance of input data in second language studies. *Language Learning* 25, 297–307.

ZAHORIK, J. 1975, Teachers' planning models. *Educational Leadership* 33, 134–9.

1 Units of Analysis in Syllabus Design — The Case for Task

MICHAEL H. LONG and GRAHAM CROOKES
University of Hawai'i

General Issues in Course Design

While rarely the case in practice, proposals for language teaching ideally involve theoretically coherent, empirically grounded choices among options in each of six areas: needs identification, syllabus design, methodology design, materials writing, testing, and program evaluation. Saying that the decisions should be theoretically coherent means that they should follow from our current understanding of how the process we are trying to facilitate works — in this case, our theory of how people learn second languages. We are obliged to have recourse to theory when making some decisions for the simple reason that, while a good deal about second language acquisition (SLA) has been discovered empirically, many aspects of what has been observed are incomplete or only partially understood. It would be preferable, of course, to base *all* the choices on empirical findings as to what works or is most effective in the classroom, but the current state of knowledge does not permit that. Where is one to begin?

As the starting point in planning courses there is much to recommend the choice of *unit of analysis* for syllabus design. It is arguably the most basic decision for two reasons. First and foremost, the option chosen, whatever it may be, will most clearly reflect the designer's (often the teacher's) theory, implicit or explicit (Ramani, 1987), of SLA. Is learning a language a matter of developing skills, learning grammar rules, building neural networks, acquiring tacit linguistic knowledge, forming new habits, becoming a member of a new culture, adding a communicative repertoire, several of these or something else? Whatever course designers or teachers think language learning involves will influence the elements of the target language they present to their students — words, structures, notions, etc. — and how

9

they should be presented — in isolation, in context, accompanied by rules, as naturally occurring parts of authentic excerpts, and so on.

A second reason for commencing with choice of the unit of analysis is that the type of syllabus chosen will have a pervasive influence on decisions in other areas, while the converse is not necessarily true. To illustrate, a program designer may decide to use either norm-referenced or criterion-referenced tests without ruling out any options in methodology or syllabus design, but choice of, say, structural or task syllabuses will *require* structures or tasks to figure in the needs assessment, methodology, materials and tests if they are not to be irrelevant or invalid. Similarly, a needs analysis conducted to identify the vocabulary and linguistic structures that learners will use in a certain occupation will obviously be compatible with a lexical or structural syllabus, respectively, but will be inadequate or unusable if the type of syllabus chosen employs notion, function, topic or task as its unit of analysis, or if the 'method' to be used, e.g. the natural approach (Krashen & Terrell, 1983), eschews a focus on language form.[1] Again, selection of a task-based (procedural, task or process) syllabus would sit well with such methodological options as communicative problem-solving activities done by students working in small groups, but would preclude classroom procedures which assume structural grading, such as most of those employed by the Audio-lingual Method, Total Physical Response, and Silent Way.

Second Language Syllabus Types

A variety of syllabus types compete for attention in the 1990s: lexical, structural, notional, functional, situational, topical, procedural, process, content-based and task, plus various multistrand combinations thereof (see McKay, 1980). It is important to note that the issue is not which particular syllabus to adopt, but which *type* and that this in turn is a question of the appropriate *unit of analysis* in syllabus design. Thus, selecting, for example, a structural syllabus, still leaves open various options as to how any particular structural syllabus will look — most obviously with regard to which structures will be *selected* for inclusion, how they will be *graded,* or sequenced, how they will be *organized,* e.g. whether structures will be recycled (so-called 'spiral' syllabuses) or presented once only in strict linear fashion, and so on. The same considerations will apply when evaluating other syllabus types. It is important to bear in mind, however, that regardless of which options are chosen in those secondary decision areas, the merit of *all* structural syllabuses will ultimately turn on the validity of morpho-syntactic structure as a unit of analysis in language learning, the process language teaching is designed to facilitate. (Note that we are not asserting the contrary position, that task is a unit of acquisition, either — see below under 'Task and three types of task-based syllabus'.)

A useful distinction to bear in mind in discussions of syllabus types is that between two superordinate categories, analytic and synthetic syllabuses (Wilkins, 1974, 1976). In *analytic* syllabuses, the

> prior analysis of the total language system into a set of discrete pieces of language that is a necessary precondition for the adoption of a synthetic approach is largely superfluous . . . Analytic approaches . . . are organized in terms of the purposes for which people are learning language and the kinds of language performance that are necessary to meet those purposes. (Wilkins, 1976: 13)

'Analytic', that is, refers not to what the syllabus designer does, but to the operations required of the learner. Wilkins goes on to say:

> since we are inviting the learner, directly or indirectly, to recognize the linguistic components of the language behaviour he is acquiring, we are in effect basing our approach on the learner's analytic capabilities. (Wilkins, 1976: 14)

Updating Wilkins' definition a little, analytic syllabuses are those that present the target language whole chunks at a time, in molar rather than molecular units, without linguistic interference or control. They rely on (a) the learners' presumed ability to perceive regularities in the input and induce rules, and/or (b) the continued availability to learners of innate knowledge of linguistic universals and the ways language can vary, knowledge which can be reactivated by exposure to natural samples of the L2. Procedural, process and task syllabuses are examples of the analytic syllabus type.[2]

In a *synthetic* language teaching 'strategy':

> different parts of language are taught separately and step by step so that acquisition is a process of gradual accumulation of parts until the whole structure of language has been built up . . . At any one time the learner is being exposed to a deliberately limited sample of language. (Wilkins, 1976: 2)

Again, 'synthetic' refers to the learner's role:

> The learner's task is to re-synthesize the language that has been broken down into a large number of small pieces with the aim of making this learning task easier. (Wilkins, 1976: 2)

Synthetic syllabuses segment the target language into discrete linguistic items, for presentation one at a time. They rely on learners' (assumed) ability to learn a language in parts (e.g. structures and functions) independently of one another, and also to integrate, or synthesize, the pieces when the time comes to use them for communicative purposes. Structural, lexical, notional, functional, and most situational and topical syllabuses are synthetic.

Wilkins argued convincingly for the conceptual distinction. He made it clear, however, that for practical purposes, he really saw analytic and synthetic syllabus types not as a dichotomy, but as the end-points on a continuum:

> . . . these approaches are not mutually exclusive . . . Any actual course or syllabus could be placed somewhere on the continuum between the wholly synthetic and the wholly analytic, but the actual decision procedures that have been followed in the process of selection will show that it tends towards one pole or the other. (Wilkins, 1976: 1–2)

A second, related, distinction is that between Type A and Type B syllabuses (White, 1988: 44–5). *Type A* syllabuses have the following characteristics. They focus on what is to be learned, the L2. They are interventionist. Someone preselects and predigests the language to be taught, dividing it up into small pieces, and determining learning objectives in advance of any consideration of who the learners may be. Type A syllabuses, therefore, White points out, are external to the learner, other-directed, determined by authority, set the teacher as decision-maker, treat the subject matter of instruction as important, assess success and failure in terms of achievement or mastery, and generally 'do things to the learner.'

Type B syllabuses, on the other hand, focus on *how* the language is to be learned. They are non-interventionist. They involve no artificial preselection or arrangement of items and allow objectives to be determined by a process of negotiation between teacher and learners after they meet, as a course evolves. They are internal to the learner, negotiated between learners and teacher as joint decision-makers, emphasize the process of learning rather than the subject matter, assess accomplishment in relationship to learners' criteria for success, and 'do things for or with the learner'. As will become clear, there is a close, but not complete, match between synthetic and analytic syllabus, on the one hand, and Type A and Type B syllabuses, on the other.

Units of Analysis in Synthetic Syllabuses

Structure

The standard works of Halliday, McIntosh & Strevens (1964) and Mackey (1965) describe what has become the orthodox approach to syllabus design concerning selection and grading in structural syllabuses. The structural syllabus consists of a series of isolated linguistic forms, or morphosyntactic 'structures', like equational sentences, yes/no and wh-questions, articles, prepositions, conditionals, and relative clauses, plus inductively or deductively presented pedagogic 'grammar points', such as when to use an infinitive or a gerund. The structures are generally presented one at a time, but occasionally in contrasting pairs, e.g. singular and plural forms of nouns, or simple present and present progressive. While structural linguistics has changed considerably over the past thirty years, the content of structural syllabuses still generally reflects the preoccupation of linguists, especially contrastivists of the 1950s and 1960s and other 'traditional, descriptive' grammarians in the 1970s and 1980s, with surface structure differences between languages. Modern generative grammar (Chomsky's universal grammar, Bresnan's Lexical Functional Grammar, Foley's lexical unification grammar, etc.) and functional–typological grammar (e.g. Givon, 1984) have as yet, at least, had little impact.

Structural syllabuses are synthetic and Type A. They are still by far the most widely used, especially in foreign language settings. Indeed, arguments in their favor remain mostly logistical. Structural syllabuses and materials, it is pointed out, are widespread and relatively easy to use, even for untrained teachers with little command of English. Change, it is claimed, would threaten such teachers and learners (not to mention textbook sales). And then there is educational gatekeeping:

> Let us now turn to a very practical argument in favor of teaching grammar, namely that many ESL/EFL students are required to pass a standardized national or international exam in order to proceed with their plans . . . Typically, a major component of such exams is grammar. Therefore, to give these students an incomplete grounding in grammar, *regardless of one's conviction about teaching it,* is to do them a great disservice. Students have to know and apply the rules of English grammar in order to do well on such tests. (Celce-Murcia & Hilles, 1988: 4, emphasis added)

Pervasive and easy to use though they may be, structural syllabuses have been criticized on several grounds. First, many have commented on the inevitable unnaturalness of structurally and lexically graded dialogs or reading passages (see, for example, Crystal, 1981; Ventola, 1987; Widdowson, 1968). Textbook characters may hold entire conversations in which all verbs are marked for the same tense and aspect, but native speakers rarely do. Second, there is a tendency to model usage, not use (Widdowson, 1971), which arises from attempts at narrow contextualization of the 'structure of the day'. This can affect teachers as well as textbook writers. A lesson on the 'present progressive', for example, may lead to model sentences native speakers would never use, such as 'I am writing on the board', said by the teacher while performing the action in full view of the class, rather than potentially authentic utterances such as 'Police are holding the man on a charge of assualt', used by a radio news reporter. A third problem is the misleading mixing of different functions of language which happen to be encoded using the same form. Widdowson (1971) notes, for example, that one may associate the imperative mood with the act of commanding, but that this is far from the whole story:

> 'Bake the pie in a slow oven', 'Come for dinner tomorrow', 'Take up his offer', 'Forgive us our trespasses'. An instruction, an invitation, advice and prayer are all different acts, yet the imperative serves them all: — and need serve none of them: 'You must bake the pie in a slow oven', 'Why don't you come to dinner tomorrow?', 'I should take up his offer', 'We pray forgiveness of our trespasses' . . . Just as one linguistic form may fulfill a variety of rhetorical functions, so one rhetorical function may be fulfilled by a variety of linguistic forms. (Widdowson, 1971: 38–9)

In addition, Wilkins (1972), among others, has drawn attention both to the negative effects on motivation for those learners who need to be able to communicate as soon as possible, and also (whether perceived as demotivating or not) the inefficiency inherent in the idea that the whole grammatical system has to be taught when few learners need it all.

Rarely mentioned but, we would argue, most serious of all, are the limitations of non-psychologically based descriptions of linguistic competence to the psychological process of SL acquisition. Full native-like syntactic constructions, for example, are unlearnable by beginners (see Cook, 1971). With no evidence and little discussion, the utility of such structures as acquisition units is typically either asserted or assumed. Yet twenty years of research on interlanguage development in and out of classrooms has shown that learners neither acquire one structure (or word, notion or function) at a time in linear, additive fashion, nor do they move from zero to native-like mastery of those items in one step, whether or not they receive error correction. Instead, they pass through apparently fixed developmental sequences in word order, negation, questions, relative clauses and so on, sequences which have to include often quite lengthy stages of *non*-target-like use of forms (as well as use of non-target forms), and which seem to be impervious to instruction. Successive stages in such sequences rarely involve single-step, non-target to full target switches, as shown, for example, by the gradual modifications marking transition through the well established four-step sequence for the acquisition of English negation by Spanish speakers (for review, see Schumann, 1979):

(1) pre-verbal (No happy. No you do that)
(2) internal preverbal, unanalysed (He not here. She no/don't have job)
(3) attachment to modal auxiliaries (I can't/mustn't go)
(4) analysed target (I don't/He doesn't/She didn't like it)

and by the frequently observed temporary 'deterioration' in learner performance (so-called 'backsliding'), which sometimes gives rise to U-shaped developmental curves (see Bowerman, 1982; Huebner, 1983; Kellerman, 1985; McLaughlin, 1988; Meisel, Clahsen & Pienemann, 1981).

Furthermore, learners do not acquire structures in isolation but as parts of complex mappings of form–function relationships. Many structures could not in principle be acquired separately, either, since they share a symbiotic relationship with others. ESL negation is intrinsically related to auxiliary development, interrogatives to word order rules, and so on. (For reviews of numerous studies supporting these generalizations, see, for example, Hatch, 1983; Ellis, 1985; Larsen-Freeman & Long, 1991.) Finally, for beginners, at least, the inadequacy of full native-like target language structure as a unit of analysis in syllabus design is further demonstrated by the consistent findings that acquisition sequences do not reflect instructional sequences (see, for example, Lightbown, 1983; Pienemann, 1987) and that while a focus on form can facilitate learning in several ways, e.g. by speeding it up (for review, see Long, 1988), it can do so only when the items chosen are appropriate to the learner's current developmental stage (Pienemann, 1984; Pienemann & Johnston, 1987). These criticisms, it should be noted, apply to synthetic syllabuses in general, not just to those employing structure as their unit of analysis.

Notion and function

The most popular alternative to have emerged to the structural syllabus is the notional (in practice, usually notional–functional) syllabus (Wilkins, 1972, 1976; compare Candlin, 1976). The notional–functional syllabus is also synthetic and Type A, but presents the target language not as isolated linguistic forms *per se,* but as groups of the linguistic devices needed to encode three kinds of semantic categories: (a) semantico-grammatical, such as time (past, present and future), place, distance, sequence, and duration; (b) modality, such as necessity, possibility, probability, and certainty; and (c) communicative function, such as offering, requesting, accusing, denying, and defining. Thus, whereas English imperatives and the modal *would* might appear far apart and unrelated in a structural syllabus, they might be grouped together in a unit of notional–functional materials, e.g. on 'Offering' ('Have another sandwich', 'Would you like another coffee?'), along with work on certain lexical items and fixed phrases (*try, how about, help yourself to*) and intonation contours frequently associated with offers.

> [A] *grammatical syllabus* is one which accords highest priority to grammatical criteria and sees the structure of language teaching as being principally provided by an ordered sequence of grammatical categories ('structures') . . . a *notional syllabus* would seek to change the balance of priorities by placing emphasis on the meanings expressed or the functions performed through language. (Wilkins, 1981: 83)

Notional–functional syllabuses are an improvement over structural ones in that materials based on them can come closer to modeling authentic target language use and can make salient the purposes to which linguistic forms are put, or their 'communicative value' (Widdowson, 1978: 11). They can also be related more visibly to students' current or future language needs, with resulting motivational benefits, although this is a function of the needs identification often conducted in preparations for notional–functional courses, not an intrinsic property of such syllabuses. Beyond this, they offer few obvious improvements, and have several flaws.

Wilkins' initial proposals have been criticized on a variety of grounds. It has been pointed out that preparation of notional syllabuses, like structural syllabuses, involves fragmenting the target language, presenting one notion or function at a time, and assuming that learners can eventually synthesize the whole, whereas functions actually co-occur in discourse, and take on communicative value from that discourse context (Crombie, 1985; Widdowson, 1978). There are also very practical problems for anyone attempting to produce a notional–functional syllabus. The set of functions is non-finite, many individual notions and functions are difficult to define or distinguish, and their linguistic exponents are often laborious to establish other than via (differing) native speaker intuitions.

It is also alleged that the notional–functional syllabus lacks a sound psychological basis. Brumfit (1981: 91–2) states that 'principles of organization must be answerable to a view of how language is learnt', but observes that Wilkins does not address himself to learning theory. Brumfit continues:

until we have some way of saying 'X is a notion and Y is not, and we can test them in the following ways', we are talking about a vacuuous concept.[3]

Wilkins' work has also been criticized for paying no attention to a theory of language acquisition and for being based purely on reasoning, not on empirical evidence (Paulston, 1981). It is certainly the case that no consideration was given to the psychological reality of notions and functions until more than a decade after their introduction (Cook, 1985).

Studies of interlanguage development provide no more support for the idea that learners acquire a language one notion or function at a time than for the idea that they do so one word or structure at a time. As Prabhu has pointed out:

[T]here are . . . methodological consequences — resulting at least in a difference of emphasis — to adopting a structural or a functional syllabus, but both kinds of syllabus have the fundamental similarity that they look on language acquisition as a planned process of input-assimilation. They both rely on the validity of the equation: what is taught = what is (or ought to be) learnt. (Prabhu, 1984: 273)

The point is moot, however, since it is the linguistic exponents of notions and functions — that is, structures, lexical items, intonation patterns, and so on — that the learner actually encounters in the input, not the notions or functions themselves. The sequencing of those items may differ from that in a structural syllabus, due to forms now being grouped according to communicative function rather than linguistic relationships or (supposed) learning difficulty. The linguistic input to and output demands on the learner, however, still typically consist of isolated native-like structures — structures which are no more plausible as instantly acquirable items for having their communicative function made more salient. In addition, reviews (e.g. Long, 1978) of commercially published notional–functional textbooks show that the exercise types, formats, and items they contain are frequently indistin- guishable from those in structurally based books (a quality by no means unique to notional–functional materials), and that their model dialogs are still far from realistic samples of the ways native speakers talk (Auerbach & Burgess, 1985; Cathcart, 1989; Pearson, 1983; Swain, 1985; Ventola, 1987; Williams, 1988).

The initial uncritical acceptance of notional–functional syllabuses was subsequently modified (Wilkins, 1974, 1981). Syllabuses, it was claimed, could range from being principally grammatical to fully notional, according to learners' needs. The role of 'an extensive mastery of the grammatical system' was reaffirmed as essential to anything more than 'a rudimentary communicative ability' (Wilkins, 1981: 85).

There is nothing new in the idea that the grammar of a language can somehow be learned, and that then communication becomes possible — nor any evidence that it is correct. As an implicit theory about how language is learned, it certainly provides a striking contrast with the claims of several first and second language acquisition researchers that grammar develops out of conversation or other language use (see, for example, Atkinson, 1979; Ervin-Tripp, 1978; Hatch, 1978; Keenan, 1974; Scollon, 1973; and for critical discussion, Sato, 1986). Nevertheless, White (1988: 78–81) notes that, perhaps as a reaction to the loss of confidence in pure notional syllabuses, hybrid structural/notional–functional syllabuses and materials have become more common in recent years, with several proposals offered for interweaving functional and structural elements (see, for example, Brumfit, 1984a; McKay, 1980; Stern, 1983; Ullman, 1982; Yalden, 1983). We would simply note that the prospects of two unmotivated units combining to produce one motivated hybrid would seem rather dim.

Situation and topic

Less well known and less widely used than structural or notional–functional varieties, two further synthetic syllabus types are those which adopt situation and topic as their unit of analysis. While one might expect that choice of these units would mean language is presented to learners in terms of where it is used and what it is used to talk, read or write about, respectively, the real picture turns out to be a little more complicated.

The term 'situational' has two possible meanings in SL syllabus design. The first, as in 'structural–situational', implies that a situational syllabus is really another variant of the basic structural kind described above. Examples of this kind of course identified by Howatt (1984: 225) are

> the audiovisual courses of CREDIF [1961] such as *Voix et Images de France* [and] a simpler adaptation popularized by L. G. Alexander in his widely used elementary course *First Things First* [1967]

and another notable example was the Australian government's so-called *Situational English* course (Commonwealth Office of Education, 1967; see Yalden (1983) for more detals of this syllabus type). Alexander (1967: xiii) actually refers to this form of 'situational' teaching as

> structurally controlled situational teaching: teaching a language by means of a series of everyday situations, while at the same time grading the structures which are presented.

In fact, however, structures are the preeminent form of sequencing here, as Alexander (1967: xvii) admits:

> In the early stages it is possible to use very few [structural] patterns indeed. This means that the 'situations' are often unconvincing and barely possible.

An example makes this indeed clear — consider the following stilted 'dialog', apparently concerning 'the garden' or, more likely, the present continuous (Alexander, 1967: 31):

Jean: Where's Sally, Jack?
Jack: She's in the garden, Jean.
Jean: What is she doing?
Jack: She's sitting under the tree.
Jean: Is Tim in the garden, too?
Jack: Yes, he is. He's climbing the tree.
Jean: I beg your pardon? Who is climbing the tree?
Jack: Tim is.
Jean: What about the dog?
Jack: The dog's in the garden, too. It's running across the grass. It's running after the cat.

The second use of 'situational' implies courses which are organized 'around situations and deal with structures as they arise' (Mohan, 1977: 251). Everyday use of the term might lead one to expect units on situations like 'At the supermarket', 'In immigration and customs', 'On vacation', or 'At the party', and such items do sometimes occur in so-called situational materials. On the basis of an analysis of representative situational course books, however, Mohan concluded that

> situational course content . . . does not consist of situations per se, but rather it consists of topics, which are illustrated by situations which show how an interaction in that topic area might develop. (Mohan, 1977: 251)

For Mohan, an example of a topic is 'shopping', under which more than one 'situation', e.g. 'shopping for food, shopping for clothes' (1977: 251) can be grouped. It is not necessarily the case that topically organized materials imply the use of situations: *English Topics* (Cook, 1974, 1978) is a collection of independent units of stimulus material and discussion questions arranged in terms of topics of general interest, intended to be used to produce classroom discussion of the topics and language which is incidental to communication and interaction in the second language. Although this kind of syllabus seems to be less popular now, there are one or two other ESL texts which are primarily topical, for example, (the somewhat confusingly titled) *Notions in English* (Jones, 1979) and *Notion by Notion* (Ferreira, 1981). Jones's text consists of a sequence of units, each of which provides the intermediate or advanced learner with material and related exercises to talk about a series of topics. Examples include the weather, shops, drinks, entertainment, money and geography. A strong synthetic undercurrent is apparent in the sub-titles to many topics, which list structural or functional items dealt with, as well as in the inclusion of overtly linguistic issues as the 'topics' (or 'notions') in several units, e.g. 'questions', 'the past', 'articles', 'isn't it?', 'word + preposition', and 'preposition + noun'. Situational aspects are purely incidental.

In general, it appears that a 'situational' syllabus often really means a 'structural–situation' syllabus, in which case it will be open to all the criticisms of structural syllabuses made earlier. True situational syllabuses and accompanying materials have been produced, however, and if often blurred in practice, situation and topic can in principle also be differentiated. Situational syllabuses have the potential advantage of tapping students' knowledge of the world as an aid to learning, and also of providing realistic, and hence motivating, materials. Topical syllabuses share this motivational potential, especially if selection is based on a needs identification performed in terms of topics or on the findings of research on frequency of topics in the conversations of people of the same age as the learner. Why, then, have they not become more widely used (at least, as indicated by the absence of published materials of this type)?

Two immediate, related difficulties when designing such syllabuses lie in defining and distinguishing situations and topics, on the one hand, and in the broadness of the concepts, with resulting lack of precision for materials design, on the other. How many separate 'situations' or 'sub-situations', for example, is a passenger involved in 'At the railway station'? Just one trip through a busy urban station in some societies might easily involve a traveller asking the way (to the ticket office, platform, restroom or snack bar), buying things (a ticket, a newspaper, a meal), decoding station announcements, reading timetables and train departure boards, dealing with porters, ticket inspectors and other passengers, and much more. Unless such additional factors as the interlocutors (ticket clerk, porter, newspaper vendor, cashier) and/or the 'immediate situation' (ticket window, newspaper kiosk, snack bar cash register, platform entrance) are also specified, it is in fact largely impossible to predict language from situation, as was elegantly argued nearly thirty years ago in a little known but important article by McIntosh (1965).

Even when more narrowly defined in these ways, however, the topics of conversations that transpire in such 'immediate situations', the notions and functions realized, and the lexical items and grammatical structures used to encode them are all still rather unpredictable. This is easily illustrated with excerpts from transcripts of approximately thirty minutes of conversations at the ticket window (a narrowly defined situation) of a small rural railroad station in Pennsylvania recorded surreptitiously several years ago by the first author in preparation for a course on English for specific purposes. The excerpts in Figure 1 were typical.

As can be seen from the samples, by no means all that transpired, even in this 'narrow situation', concerned either trains or the purchase of tickets, and when tickets were involved, terms like *one-way, bargain, tripper* and *senior* were preferred to the less informative *ticket.* Perhaps coincidentally, one of the few to use *ticket,* passenger D, was a non-native speaker. Most exchanges involved sales of other items (candy, newspapers, cigarettes, etc.) also handled by the clerk, and/or personal matters (the fate of a lost dog the previous day, an illegally parked car, and so on). The appropriacy of these items was no doubt partly determined by the small size of the station, the suburban location, the familiarity of the interlocutors (ticket clerk and, for the most part, regular commuters), and other factors. The kinds of constructions modeled for passengers in situational language teaching materials for such occasions, however — 'How much is a ticket to Liverpool?', 'Which platform does the train to London leave from?' or 'I'd like a window seat, please' (see Cross, 1980) — would be just as atypical and inappropriate at the front of the line at a ticket window in a busy urban terminus, and during rush hour, at least in some countries, considerably more likely to elicit abuse (or worse) from fellow passengers and ticket clerk alike.

A further problem with situational (indeed, all) syllabuses, is grading. There is in principle no way to grade situations in terms of difficulty or as to which ones need to be 'learned' before others, as should be obvious from the previous discussion of the more fundamental problem of specifying situations themselves or the language that occurs in them. (See Bell (1981a) for further discussion.) Commenting on this issue, McKay (1980) observes that

> some [situational] syllabuses (e.g. Georgetown University A.L.I., 1968) are ordered on the basis that the learner will encounter the situations (e.g. a text for foreign students might proceed as follows; landing at the airport, finding a place to live, registering at the university, etc.). Other situational texts . . . rely on the structural complexity of the dialogues for the sequencing of the material. (McKay, 1980: 76)

McKay cites *Let's Talk* (Finocchiaro, 1970) as an example of the latter (structural) approach to grading (situations).

A.

How you doin'?

Tripper?

(2) That's Bethayres to Logan?

(8) (XXX)

[stamps ticket] (5)
OK   Eleven she be
and
Thank you

Alright and yourself?

Right

Right

Mmhm

Right

B.

Morning   Yes (mam)

OK   That'll be one-twenty

[giving change] That'll be two

OK

Yes   There's an eight fifty-
two due next   Then comes the
nine o one

Morning   Senior citizen one
way   Terminal   (By the way)

[gives money]

(Thank you)

(5) [returning to counter] Is
there a train expected before
the nine o one?

Thank you

C.

I need a couple of bargains
Did you get rid of the doggie?

Yeah   I had to finally send
him away   (He) was here until
eleven o'clock (and) no
body
claimed him so (2)   OK

Really?

[holding up cigarettes and and
candy] Three seventy and
twenty-five

Right   right
Mmhm

Ok

D.

Nine o one train's passed yet?

No not yet

Not yet?   Ah   (xx)

Ok what would you like?

(6) Five bargain ticket [*sic*] please

[stamps ticket]   That'll be nine twenty-(seven)

[gives money]

That'll be ten   Thank you

(Is it) OK that my blue car is parked (in front of here)? (2) In front (1) In the uh (xx) Here is the Volkswagen?

Yeah well that's-
Well I don't know   That's for handicapped
people (there xx)

Red Volkswagen?

Oh OK   I'm gonna put (it) park over there

FIGURE 1   *At the ticket window*

In sum, to take situation as the unit of analysis in a synthetic syllabus is problematic because most situations are too ill-defined and too broad to be used in identifying learner needs, designing materials or testing. Where you use language, it also turns out, is less relevant for language learning than what you use it for, i.e. *task*. While not without problems itself, task comes closer to providing a basis for all those aspects of course design, as we shall see.

Many of the criticisms of situational syllabuses apply to topical syllabuses, too. Topic is also a broad, difficult to define, semantic construct (for discussion, see Brown & Yule, 1983; Sirois & Dorval, 1988), and like situations, topics have an unfortunate tendency to merge into one another (Goodenough & Weiner, 1978; Jefferson, 1978) and subsume other topics (van Oosten, 1984).[4]

A further drawback is that, like situation, topic is of limited use for predicting grammatical form, although it does slightly better with vocabulary. A discussion of a particular TESOL Convention could well involve a variety of genres such as explanations, opinions, narratives, reports and so on, which in turn require a vast range of lexis and linguistic constructions to be encoded. Even an apparently 'narrower' topic, like 'next Sunday's American football game', might easily involve the specialized jargon of rules, equipment and strategies for playing the game, famous games, clubs and players, last Sunday's game, another upcoming game, a commentary on a game, old knee injuries, the money involved, the NFL players' union, drug abuse, racial discrimination, and so on. As with situations, there is also no obvious way to grade or sequence topics, given the impossibility of distinguishing their boundaries or predicting what they involve.

Word

Among the earliest efforts to provide SL teaching with some empirical support are the various vocabulary selection studies, which were influential in the 1920s and 1930s (Faucett, West, Palmer & Thorndike, 1936; Ogden, 1930; West, 1926). Initiated in Prussia for the training of stenographers, vocabulary frequency studies were seen as an obvious way of ensuring that students learned the most 'important' words first. The manifestations of these projects varied. Ogden's *Basic English* was intended as an auxiliary language and will be remembered for contributing 'doublethink' to the language (via George Orwell). The joint work of British and American specialists (Faucett *et al.*, 1936) became known as the Carnegie List, and was utilized in a major text whose popularity lasted until the 1960s: *Essential English* (Eckersley, 1938–42). (For further details, see Widdowson, 1968; Howatt, 1984.)

Recent advances in techniques for the computer analysis of large data bases of authentic text have helped resuscitate this line of work. The modern lexical syllabus is discussed in Sinclair & Renouf (1988), and related work on collocation is reported by Sinclair (1987) and Kennedy (1989). The *Collins COBUILD English Course* (Willis & Willis, 1988) is cited as an exemplary pedagogic implementation of the work. In fact, however, the COBUILD textbooks utilize one of the more complex hybrid syllabuses in current ESL texts. Seven strands refer to: (1) tasks and topics, (2) texts and features, (3) writing, (4) social language, (5) verbs/tenses and clause patterns, (6) noun phrases, pronouns, adjectives, prepositions and adverbial phrases, and (7) spoken and written discourse. The objectives for each unit are grouped under three categories: (a) lexical, (b) grammar and discourse, and (c) tasks. Many tasks, however, look like 'macro' functions, e.g. (in Book 1), talking about families, describing things, expressing likes and dislikes, discussing and comparing buildings, and explaining answers.

In their introduction to the *Teacher's Book,* Willis & Willis (1988, ii–vi) are refreshingly open and explicit about what they are attempting to achieve. The methodology for the Course, the reader is informed, adheres to five basic principles:

1 People learn a language most effectively by using the language to do things — to find out information, to solve problems, to talk about personal experiences, and so on.
2 A focus on accuracy is vital.
3 As far as possible learners should be exposed to real language.
4 Grammar is learned rather than taught. Coursebooks and teachers provide useful guidelines on the language, but learners should additionally be encouraged to think and deduce for themselves.
5 Learners need strategies for organising what they have learned — they need rules, patterns and categories.

> The *Collins COBUILD English Course* realises these well-established principles through a new language syllabus — a lexical syllabus . . . (Willis & Willis, 1988, ii)

The sense of a potential conflict between some of these principles, e.g. 1, 3 and 4, on the one hand, and 2 and 5, on the other, is strengthened by the information (p. iii) that the 'syllabus for Level One consists of 700 of the commonest words in today's English', for it would seem unlikely that 'real language' will happen to be lexically graded in this way. Similarly, a two-stage classroom procedure the authors describe for student work on pedagogic tasks, although obviously carefully thought out, assumes that students can simultaneously work towards task accomplishment and target-like performance of the code. Problem-solving tasks of various kinds are first to be done in small groups, where the 'focus is not on the language itself, but on the performing of the task in order to reach the desired outcome' (p. iii). The task, however, 'is not the final goal of the teaching cycle' (p. iii). A public report to the whole class is to follow, and because it is public and potential input for other learners, 'it is appropriate that the report should be accurate as well as fluent' (p. iii). Finally, in addition to student study of texts to find particular language features, there is controlled practice:

> Controlled repetition of various kinds involves students in the practising of useful and very frequent combinations of words in English, in order sounds and intonation patterns accurately and spontaneously. (Willis & Willis, 1988: iv)

The COBUILD Course offers what appear to be some of the most 'authentic' texts and dialogs in commercially published language teaching materials. The exercises and pedagogic tasks are attractively presented, stimulating, and carefully planned, and the whole package looks user-friendly. We are not persuaded, however, that these accomplishments (assuming our assessments are accurate) have anything to do with the Course (supposedly) being based on a lexical syllabus, as opposed to the ingenuity of the authors (Willis & Willis), the insights of the COBUILD project's leader (Sinclair), and the extensive field testing that preceded the materials' publication.

According to Sinclair & Renouf (1988), the main benefit of a lexical syllabus is that it emphasizes utility — the student learns that which is most valuable because it is most frequent. This is part of the rationale for any needs analysis (see West, 1926), however, so one may ask whether identifying needs in terms of lexical frequency provides any special benefit. Sinclair & Renouf claim that working from the lexical end of language selection acts as a shortcut to the correct selection of other linguistic material. Holding that modern SL syllabuses ignore content, and that notional/functional syllabuses, for example, are 'incomplete', they remark that

> if the analysis of the words and phrases has been done correctly then all the relevant grammar, etc. [i.e. structures, notions, and functions] should appear in a proper proportion. (Sinclair & Renouf, 1988: 155)

This interesting claim is unfortunately not supported with any evidence. In addition, it is asserted that the lexical syllabus is 'neutral' with regard to 'the use of tasks to practice effective communication', since it is 'an independent syllabus, unrelated by any principles to any methodology' (p. 155), and that indeed, all syllabuses should be independent of methodology (p. 145). It is, therefore, subject to the same criticism leveled by Brumfit against notional/functional syllabuses, that it (in this case, deliberately) takes no cognizance of how a second language is learned. (For further discussion see Long & Crookes, 1992.) It is in addition threatened by other general problems of synthetic syllabuses, to which we now turn.

Generic problems with synthetic syllabuses

Whatever the unit of analysis — structure, notion, function, situation, topic or word — synthetic syllabuses share a static, target language, product orientation. Syllabus content is ultimately based on an analysis of the *language* to be learned, whether this be overt, as in the case of structure, word, notion, and function, or covert, as has usually been the case with situation and topic. Further, the analysis is conducted on an idealized native speaker version of that language. It is assumed that the unit, or teaching point, which is presented will be what is learned, and that it is efficient to organize and present material in an isolating fashion. SLA research offers no evidence to suggest that any of these synthetic units are meaningful acquisition units, that they are (or even can be) acquired separately, singly, in linear fashion, or that they can be learned prior to and separate from language use. In fact, the same literature provides overwhelming evidence against all those tacit assumptions.

SLA is sufficiently difficult that most learners' attempts end in at least partial failure. Whatever the relative merits of one unit compared to another, therefore, the psychological processes involved in learning would seem to have priority over arguments concerning alternative ways of analyzing the ideal, but rarely attained, product. While it also involves the acquisition of social and cultural knowledge, language learning is a psycholinguistic process, not a linguistic one, yet synthetic syllabuses consistently leave the learner out of the equation.

Units of Analysis in Analytic Syllabuses

Early proposals

Whereas synthetic syllabuses are concerned mostly with the language to be taught, alternatives accord as much or more attention to learners and language learning. Both analytic and Type B syllabuses are based on the view that language (like other cognitive skills, see Crookes, 1991; Levelt, 1978; Welford, 1968) is something that may be acquired by analysis, rather than through a process of accretion. The position goes back at least 300 years (see Howatt, 1984), but was more recently articulated by Newmark (1966: 77): 'if the task of learning to speak English were additive and linear . . . it is difficult to see how anyone could learn [it] . . .'. Newmark maintained that 'language is learned a whole act at a time, rather than as an assemblage of constituent skills'.[5] He conceived of a language course of an 'analytic' type, where large 'chunks' of language were presented and learned, the presentation possibly on videotape, the learning through observation, and practice through extensive use of roleplay (see Candlin, 1972). Newmark & Reibel (1968) and Reibel (1969) argued for the irrelevance to what was known about language learning of traditional approaches to sequencing. They claimed that even if done correctly, the result could be only a series of texts whose linguistic properties might collectively reflect real language use (in which case, why not use authentic texts?), but any one of which would be a distorted sample and, hence, a potential hindrance to learning.[6]

Early proposals concerning analytic, Type B, syllabuses (Macnamara, 1973; Newmark, 1964, 1966; Newmark & Reibel, 1968; Reibel, 1969) had little institutional backing and no accompanying teaching materials distributed by large commercial publishers, both factors which inhibit the spread of ideas in language teaching, good or bad (Richards, 1984a). Not surprisingly, therefore, classroom implementation was initially small scale and the result of individual effort and imagination (Allwright, 1976; Dakin, 1973; Newmark, 1971). One somewhat larger institutionalized project was reported, however, in connection with development of the Malaysian Language Syllabus (Kementerian Pelajaran Malaysia, 1975).

The Malaysian case obviously antedates most of the theoretical work discussed so far. Original implementation was influenced by the British 'communicative approach' to language teaching and specifically the early 1970s (L1) materials development work of Sinclair (discussed in Howatt, 1984: 279–80). Throughout the materials related to this program, the term 'activity' is used, and we consider it under the general heading of 'analytic'.

Following governmental specification in 1975 of three simple program goals, 24 general objectives were listed by program developers, and the political, business and educational establishments were asked to add to, delete from or otherwise modify the list. The revised version was taken to constitute a needs analysis (Richards, 1984b), and used as the basis for constructing English language 'products'. (For further details, see Rodgers, 1984; Samah, 1984.) An example of an objective was to 'follow and understand a talk on specific topics', and an example of a 'classroom procedure': 'A foreign visitor has expressed interest in a poster showing local tourist attractions. Describe the attractions shown on the poster' (Malaysian English Language Syllabus, 1975, cited in Richards, 1984b: 36). No systematic evaluation of the program was ever carried out, and for reasons which appear to have been largely institutional, use of the syllabus was discontinued (Etherton, 1979; Rodgers, 1979).

It is only recently that some more substantial attempts to use analytic syllabuses have appeared. While situation and topic could in principle be used as units of analysis in that work, this has not happened. Most attempts to date have chosen task as the unit of analysis. Definitions of task have varied, however, and three very different kinds of task-based syllabuses have emerged: procedural, process, and task. Reflecting their (predominantly) Type B, as opposed simply to analytic, orientation, all three proposals devote explicit attention to the learning or language learning process and how best to facilitate it, and each goes at least some way towards offering an integrated approach to program design, not just syllabus design.

Task and Three Types of Task-based Syllabus

Procedural syllabuses

The procedural syllabus is associated with the work of Prabhu, Ramani and others (then) at the Regional Institute of English in Bangalore, India. The Bangalore/Madras Communicational Teaching Project (Prabhu, 1980, 1984, 1987) was implemented in eight classrooms with some 18 teachers and 390 children aged 8 to 15, for periods of one to three years, from 1979 to 1984. Early influences were similar to those of the Malaysian communicative syllabuses, but were quickly abandoned:

> Communicative teaching in most Western thinking has been training *for* communication, which I claim involves one in some way or other in preselection; it is a kind of matching of notion and form. Whereas the Bangalore Project is teaching *through* communication; and therefore the very notion of communication is different. (Prabhu, 1980: 164)

Prabhu disagrees with several aspects of Monitor Theory (as in Krashen, 1982), including the idea that comprehensible input is an adequate methodological construct. However, he supports the idea that students need plenty of opportunity to develop their comprehension abilities before any production is demanded of them, he recognizes that acquisition of a linguistic structure is not 'an instant, one-step procedure', and he claims (Prabhu, 1984, 1987) with Krashen that language form is acquired subconsciously through 'the operation of some internal system of abstract rules and principles' when the learner's attention is focused on meaning, i.e. task-completion, not language (Prabhu, 1987: 70). This view of the learning process shows that a procedural syllabus is clearly of an analytic nature:

> any attempt to guide that process more directly (and whether or not explicitly) is rejected as being unprofitable and probably harmful. There is therefore no syllabus in terms of vocabulary or structure, no preselection of language items for any given lesson or activity and no stage in the lesson when language items are practised or sentence production as such is demanded. The basis of each lesson is a problem or a task . . . (Prabhu, 1984: 275–6)

Prabhu's definition of 'task' for the purposes of the Bangalore project was fairly abstract, and oriented towards cognition, process and (teacher-fronted) pedagogy:

> An activity which required learners to arrive at an outcome from given information through some process of thought, and which allowed teachers to control and regulate that process, was regarded as a 'task'. (Prabhu, 1987: 24)

In practice, two related tasks or two versions of the same task were typically paired. The first, or 'pre-task', was used by the teacher in a whole-class format, perhaps with one or more pupils. Its purpose was to present and demonstrate the task, to assess its difficulty for the class (if necessary, to modify it accordingly), and perhaps most crucial of all, for what Prabhu (1984: 276) describes vaguely as 'to let the language relevant to it come into play'. The second, the task proper, was for the pupils to work on, usually individually. There followed feedback from the teacher on task accomplishment.

Tasks in a procedural syllabus should be intellectually challenging enough to maintain students' interest, for that is what will sustain learners' efforts at task completion, focus them on meaning and, as part of that process, engage them in confronting the task's linguistic demands (Prabhu, 1987: 55–7). Opinion-gap, and later, information-gap and (especially) reasoning-gap activities were favored in the Bangalore project (for discussion, see Prabhu, 1987: 46–53). It is important that learners perceive a task as presenting a 'reasonable challenge', i.e. as difficult, but feasible. Difficulty is initially a matter of trial and error, and 'a rough measure of reasonable challenge for us is that at least half the class should be successful with at least half the task' (Prabhu, 1984: 277).

Prabhu (1987: 138–43) provides a list of the 'task types' (how tasks were classified is far from obvious) that pupils worked on in the Bangalore project, of which the following are representative:

> Tabular information: Interpreting information presented in tables e.g. about books (columns for title, author, publisher, price, year of publication); applicants for a job (columns for age, qualifications, past employment); also schools, hotels, etc.

> Distances: Working out the distances between places, from given distances between other places or from the scale of a map, comparing distances and deciding on desirable routes of travel in given situations, constructing maps from distances and directions inferred from given descriptions.

> Stories and dialogues: Listening to stories (of a 'whodunit' kind) and completing them with appropriate solutions, reading stories or dialogues and answering comprehension questions (particularly of an inferential kind) on them . . . identifying factual inconsistencies in given narrative or descriptive accounts. (Prabhu, 1987: 46–7)

As these examples suggest, Bangalore tasks were mostly of the kind familiar in the many variants of so-called 'communicative language teaching' (CLT) which emerged in Europe in the 1970s. CLT is not 'task-based' in the analytic sense, but sometimes employs problem-solving 'communication' activities in the 'practice phase' of lessons or as a means of covering the linguistic items of various kinds which still make up the covert syllabus content (see, for example, Madden & Reinhart, 1987; Nunan, 1989). That is, activities in the Bangalore Project were pre-set *pedagogic tasks,* not related to a set of *target tasks* determined by an analysis of a particular group of learners' future needs.

The radical departure from CLT the Bangalore Project represented lay, then, not in the tasks themselves (see Greenwood (1985) for a brief critique), but in the accompanying pedagogic focus on task completion instead of on the language used in the process. Two of the more salient innovations concerned the kind of input to which pupils were exposed and the absence of overt feedback on error. With respect to input, teacher speech accompanying use of a procedural syllabus is not preselected or structurally graded, but 'roughly tuned' as a natural by-product of the spontaneous adjustments made to communicate with less proficient speakers inside or outside classrooms (Prabhu, 1987: 57–9). Where errors are concerned, ungrammatical learner utterances are accepted for their content, although they may be reformulated by the teacher (what Prabhu, (1987: 61) calls 'incidental', as opposed to 'systematic', correction) in the same way that a caretaker reacts to the truth value of a child's speech and provides 'off-record' corrective feedback in the process. In these and other areas, Prabhu's pedagogic proposals are strikingly similar to those of the Natural Approach (Krashen & Terrell, 1983).

Presumably in part because of prevailing local cultural and educational norms and practices rather than any inherent property of procedural syllabuses, most other aspects of classroom instruction in the Bangalore Project were quite traditional. There was considerable emphasis on 'receptive language', classes were 'teacher-centered', group work was discouraged 'because of the fear that learner–learner interaction will promote fossilization' (Prabhu, 1987: 82), and there was little or no student–student communication. The avoidance of group work because of concerns over degenerate input, in particular, seems to have been unduly conservative in light of the research findings on interlanguage talk, which suggest that (unless peer talk is the *only* source of input) stabilization need not be a concern and that any such risk is outweighed by the opportunities for negotiation work possible, given the right task types (for review, see Long & Porter, 1985; Pica, 1987b).

Despite being an interesting, innovative program, and all the more praiseworthy for having been carried out under difficult teaching conditions, the Bangalore Project has been criticized, even by sympathetic observers (see, for example, Brumfit, 1984b). One of the chief complaints has been its failure to build an evaluation component into the design (a criticism rarely made of programs using synthetic syllabuses). In an attempt to remedy this, Beretta (1986) and Beretta & Davies (1985) reported a *post hoc* comparison of intact groups, four project classes and four roughly comparable classes in the same schools which had been taught using the traditional structurally based program. It was found that the four traditionally taught groups out-performed project classes on a discrete-point structure test, whereas three out of four project groups did statistically significantly better on tests of listening and reading comprehension, and all four better on a 'task-based' test modeled closely on the kind of (reasoning-gap) inferencing tasks used extensively with the project group students. The evaluators recognized that comparison groups had not been formed randomly, and also reported that three out of four experimental groups had had 'better qualified, more highly motivated teachers' and were accustomed to being observed and treated as 'guinea-pigs' (Beretta & Davies, 1985: 123). They suggested, nevertheless, that the test results were not unfavorable to the Bangalore Project.

More important than any shortcomings in the way this particular program was implemented (see Beretta, 1989, 1990; Prabhu, 1990a, 1990b), we would suggest, is whether or not procedural syllabuses as advocated by Prabhu are *in principle* well motivated. The procedural syllabus in its present form presents at least three difficulties:

1. In the absence of a task-based (or, indeed, any) needs identification, no rationale exists for the content of such a syllabus, i.e. for task selection. Tasks may or may not appear to have been well conceived, but it is impossible for anyone (program staff or critics, alike) to verify the appropriateness of particular pedagogic tasks for a given group of learners without objective evaluation criteria, one of which must surely be relevance to learner needs.

2. Grading task difficulty and sequencing tasks both appear to be arbitrary processes, left partly to real-time impressionistic judgments by the classroom teacher. Use of a '50% of the task by half the class' (or any such) criterion for assessing difficulty is not a satisfactory solution, for it makes task achievement a norm-referenced issue, reveals nothing about what made one task 'easier' than another, and thereby precludes any generalizations to new materials. Moreover, if the presence of a (pedagogic) task in a syllabus is justified (non-arbitrary) at all, as we assume it should be, then a criterion-referenced approach is called for. The passing grade might vary somewhat,[7] but if a task is a necessary part of the syllabus, it is presumably necessary for all students.

3. There are (1) logical arguments having to do with the need for *in*comprehensible input and communication breakdowns if learners are to perceive negative evidence as such in SLA (see, e.g. Bley-Vroman, 1986; White, 1987), (2) arguments for the importance of noticing input–output mismatches for learning to take place (Schmidt, 1990, 1993), and (3) empirical findings on interlanguage development (for review, see Long, 1988), which support the need for a *focus on form* in language teaching, yet this is proscribed in Prabhu's (as in Krashen's) work.

Process syllabuses

A second task-based approach to course design is the process syllabus (Breen & Candlin, 1980; Breen, 1984, 1987a,b; Candlin, 1984, 1987; Candlin & Murphy, 1987). The early rationale for process syllabuses was educational and philosophical, not psycholinguistic, with curriculum design proposals for other subject areas (e.g. Freire, 1970; Stenhouse, 1975) constituting an important influence. Type A syllabuses were rejected for their interventionist, authoritarian nature:

> targets for language learning are all too frequently set up externally to learners with little reference to the value of such targets in the general educational development of the learner. (Candlin, 1987: 16–17)

A social and problem-solving orientation, with explicit provision for the expression of individual learning styles and preferences, is favored over a view of teaching as the transmission of preselected and predigested knowledge. This outlook is reflected in Candlin's rather formidable definition of task as:

> one of a set of differentiated, sequencable, problem-posing activities involving learner and teachers in some joint selection from a range of varied cognitive and communicative procedures applied to existing and new knowledge in the collective exploration and pursuance of foreseen or emergent goals within a social milieu. (Candlin, 1987: 10).

Breen & Candlin's focus was and is the learner and learning processes and preferences, not the language or language-learning processes. They argue that any syllabus, preset or not, is constantly subject to negotiation and reinterpretations by teachers and learners in the classroom. In a very real sense, Candlin (1984) suggests, what a syllabus really consists of can only be discerned after a course is over, by observing not what was planned, but what took place. Both Breen and Candlin claim that learning should be and can only be the product of negotiation, and that it is the negotiation process itself that drives learning, including language learning. Hence: 'a Process

Syllabus addresses the overall question: "Who does what with whom, on what subject-matter, with what resources, when, how, and for what learning purpose(s)?'" (Breen, 1984: 56).

Breen (1984) advocates replacement of the traditional conception of the syllabus as a list of items making up a *repertoire of* communication by one which promotes a learner's *capacity for* communication:

> . . . the emphasis would be upon the capabilities of applying, reinter-preting, and adapting the knowledge of rules and conventions during communication by means of underlying skills and abilities. In other words, an emphasis on knowing *how* to participate in target language communication. Of course, knowing 'what' and 'how' are interdependent; being able to share meanings entails and refines our knowledge of the systems through which meaning is conveyed. However, the *emphasis* of conventional syllabus design has been upon systems of knowledge external to learners rather than upon skills and abilities which learners initially bring to communication, and which they have to engage during communication. (Breen, 1984: 52)

Breen talks of incorporating a content syllabus within a process syllabus as an 'external check' on what students are supposed to know, but he is clear that procedural knowledge is to replace declarative knowledge as the primary element in syllabus content, and process is to replace product:

> . . . conventional syllabus design has oriented toward language as primary subject matter . . . An alternative orientation would be towards the subject-matter of *learning* a language. This alternative provides a change of focus from content for learning towards the process of learning in the classroom situation. (Breen, 1984: 52)

The process syllabus is a plan for incorporating the negotiation process, and thereby, learning processes, into syllabus design. As described by Breen (1984), it embodies a hierarchical model, specifying sets of options at four levels, final selection among which at each level is left for users to decide on. Course design consists of providing the resources and materials needed for (1) making general decisions about classroom language learning (who needs to learn what, how they prefer to learn it, when, with whom, and so on), (2) alternative procedures for making those decisions (the basis for an eventual 'working contract' between teacher and learners), (3) alternative activities, such as teacher-led instruction, group work and laboratory use (for detail, see Breen, Candlin & Waters, 1979), and (4) alternative tasks, i.e. a bank of pedagogic tasks students may select from to realize the 'activities':

[I]t is at the level of tasks that the actual working process of the classroom group is realized in terms of what is overtly done from moment to moment within the classroom. (Examples at task level would include such things as agreeing on a definition of a problem, organizing data, deducing a particular rule or pattern, discussing reactions, etc.). (Breen, 1984: 56)

Finally, procedures are provided for formative evaluation of the effectiveness of options chosen at levels (2), (3) and (4) in accomplishing the goals agreed upon at level (1). Breen defines task as:

any structured language learning endeavor which has a particular objective, appropriate content, a specified working procedure, and a range of outcomes for those who undertake the task. 'Task' is therefore assumed to refer to a range of workplans which have the overall purpose of facilitating language learning — from the simple and brief exercise type, to more complex and lengthy activities such as group problem-solving or simulations and decision making. (Breen, 1987a: 23)

Published criticisms of the process syllabus (see, for example, Kouraogo, 1987; White, 1988) claim that it lacks a formal field evaluation, assumes an unrealistically high level of competence in both teachers and learners, and implies a redefinition of role relationships and a redistribution of power and authority in the classroom that would be too radical and/or culturally unacceptable in some societies. The need it creates for a wide range of materials and learning resources is also noted to be difficult to provide for and to pose a threat to traditional reliance, however undesirable, on a single textbook, which *is* the syllabus for most teachers, learners and examiners.

While understandable, these are concerns about the logistical feasibility of implementing process syllabuses in certain contexts, not flaws in the process syllabus itself. As such, they are not especially pertinent. After all, one would hardly fault radiography as a treatment for cancer because it is unusable without medical expertise, consenting patients and electricity. Moreover, skepticism about peoples' desire and ability to take control of their own learning is to ignore the success of educational programs of all sorts where learners from different cultural backgrounds have done exactly that, often under the most adverse circumstances (see, e.g. Freire, 1970, 1972; Hirshon, 1983; MacDonald, 1985; Vilas, 1986), as well as 200 years of successful libertarian education (see, for example, Avrich, 1980; Holt, 1972; Illich, 1971; Spring, 1975; and issues of *Libertarian Education*).

More problematic, in our view, are some of the same weaknesses which we claimed were likely to limit the effectiveness of the procedural syllabus and which we think are inherent in process syllabuses.

1. Like procedural syllabuses, process syllabuses deal in pedagogic tasks whose availability (in the task 'bank') is not based on any prior needs identification, which raises problems for selection. We recognize that prespecification of syllabus content is precisely what Breen and Candlin seek to avoid, and accept that prespecification both in syllabuses and in the commercially published materials that embody them suffers from all the weaknesses they allege (in addition to their lack of psycholinguistic credibility). We think, however, that arbitrary selection is due to the lack of a needs identification, not to prespecification *per se*. Moreover, while some learners (and teachers) might in practice recognize which tasks were relevant to their future needs (assuming such tasks happened to have been included in the task 'bank') and choose to work on them, course designers have a responsibility to ensure that use of class time is as efficient and as relevant as possible, and that a (task-based) needs identification can help achieve that.

    Preselecting pedagogic tasks on the basis of pre-identified target tasks need not mean that learner choices in other areas, such as methodology, are curtailed, although it does admittedly mean limiting the choice of tasks available. Nor need it restrict options provided at other levels in Breen's model. To use a medical analogy, we would like to have patients able to choose from among a range of alternative treatments, but expect the physician to limit their choice to remedies for what ails them. We assume, of course, that a properly conducted needs identification makes course designers better at diagnosing learner needs (as opposed to wants) than learners themselves, an assumption which is routinely accepted in the provision of all other professional services we can think of (the medical being an obvious case), but recognize that this is neither inevitably true nor universally accepted where language teaching is concerned — a fact that ought to provoke serious consideration of its often-claimed status as a profession.[8]

2. Grading task difficulty and sequencing tasks are discussed by Candlin (1987), where a variety of possible criteria are put forward, without any resolution. This is a valid reflection of the state of the art (see Crookes (1986), Nunan (1989) and Robinson (1990) for discussion of these issues), but a problem for the process syllabus (and all task-based syllabuses), nonetheless.

3. A focus on language form is not addressed in prescriptions for the procedural syllabus. Given SLA findings discussed earlier, this is a weakness.

4. It is not clear to what (if any) theory or research in SLA the process syllabus is to be held accountable, as there is relatively little reference to the *language*-learning literature in the writing on process syllabuses. This may be a reaction to the tendency for SLA theorists to ignore general education literature when making proposals for language education. However, given the evidence for at least some uniqueness for language competence and acquisition, and given the range of theories developed to account for it, it is difficult to evaluate proposals concerning the organization of SL learning which have not been linked to this body of knowledge.

Task-based language teaching

A third approach to course design which takes task as the unit of analysis is task-based language teaching (Long, 1985, 1989, to appear; Crookes, 1986; Crookes & Long, 1987; Long & Crookes, 1987, 1992). Task-based language teaching (TBLT) bases arguments for an analytic, Type B, syllabus on what is currently known about the processes involved in second language learning (see, for example, Hatch, 1983; Ellis, 1985; Larsen-Freeman & Long, 1991), on the findings of second language classroom research (see, for example, Chaudron, 1988), and on principles of course design made explicit in the 1970s, chiefly in EFL contexts, for the teaching of languages for specific purposes (e.g. Mackay & Mountford, 1978; Selinker, Tarone & Hanzeli, 1981; Swales, 1985, 1990; Tickoo, 1988; Widdowson, 1979).

A review of descriptive and experimental studies comparing tutored and naturalistic acquisition of SL morphology and syntax suggests that formal instruction (1) has little or no effect on developmental sequences, (2) possibly has a positive quantitative effect on the use of some learning strategies, as indicated by the relative frequencies of certain error types in tutored and untutored learners, (3) clearly has a positive effect on rate of learning, and (4) probably improves the ultimate level of SL attainment (Long, 1988). Moreover, the advantages for instructed learners cannot be explained as the result of those learners having received more or better comprehensible input, which is necessary, but insufficient (cf. Krashen, 1985), for major aspects of SLA. Rather, while most current treatment of language as object is undoubtedly wasted for being unusable by learners at the time it occurs, drawing learners' attention to certain classes of linguistic elements in the input does appear to facilitate development in several ways when certain conditions are met.

To illustrate, the following are five examples of how a *focus on form* may help SLA, each of which has some empirical support. Instruction in marked or more marked L2 forms may transfer to implied unmarked or less marked items (Doughty, 1991; Eckman, Bell & Nelson, 1988; Zobl, 1985). Giving increased salience to non-salient or semantically opaque grammatical features may decrease the time needed for learners to notice them in the input (Schmidt, 1990, Schmidt & Frota, 1986). Increased planning may promote use of more complex language and, possibly, of developmentally more advanced interlingual forms (Crookes, 1989). Instruction targeted at an appropriate level may speed up passage through a developmental sequence and extend the scope of application of a new rule (Pienemann & Johnston, 1987). Overt feedback on error targeted at an appropriate level and *in*comprehensible input (two kinds of negative evidence) may help destabilize an incorrect rule and may even be crucial for this to happen, as in cases where the L2 is more restrictive in a given linguistic domain (White, 1989). For example, a learner's L1 may allow two options in adverb placement, subject–verb agreement after collective nouns, or subject pronoun suppliance in discoursally marked and unmarked contexts, and the L2 only one of those options. While only one of the rules is correct when transferred to the L2, however, both may be communicatively successful with L2 speakers, with the result that the untutored learner may not receive negative feedback (because the error never causes a breakdown in communication) and so never realizes that the form is ungrammatical.

If correct, Long's (1988) conclusions, combined with these and other potential explanations of *how* instructed learners come to outperform naturalistic learners, support systematic provision for a *focus on form* in the design of language teaching. That is, systematic use will be made of pedagogic tasks and other methodological options which draw students' attention to certain aspects of the target language code. *Which* aspects of the language, when, how, and for which learners, need to be specified in more detail, of course. The five examples above offer some suggests. Long (to appear) proposes additional ways in which learner production, both grammatical and ungrammatical, can provide teachers with cues as to when it is (in)appropriate for teachers temporarily to interrupt work on a pedagogic task to focus students' attention on form.

If correct, the same conclusions about the effects of instruction do *not*, however, support a return to a *focus on forms* (plural) in language teaching, that is, to the use of some kind of synthetic syllabus and/or a linguistically isolating teaching 'method', such as ALM, Silent Way or TPR. A focus on form*s* is ruled out for all the arguments offered earlier against analytic Type A, syllabuses. Most important in this regard is the evidence from SLA research of the need to respect 'learner syllabuses' (Corder, 1967) and the related evidence against full native speaker target code forms as viable acquisition units, at the very least where beginners are concerned.

Against this background, Long and Crookes adopt task as the unit of analysis in an attempt to provide an integrated, internally coherent approach to all six phases of program design, one which is compatible with current SLA theory. There is no suggestion that learners acquire a new language one task at a time, any more than they do (say) one structure at a time. It is claimed, rather, that (pedagogic) tasks provide a vehicle for the presentation of appropriate target language samples to learners — input which they will inevitably reshape via application of general cognitive processing capacities — and for the delivery of comprehension and production opportunities of negotiable difficulty. New form–function relationships in the target language are perceived by the learner as a result. The strengthening of the subset of those that are not destabilized by negative feedback, their increased accessibility and incorporation in more intricate associations within long-term memory, complexifies the grammar and constitutes SL development.

Many target tasks (e.g. asking the way or requesting landing permission) require language use, many (e.g. digging a trench or cooking vegetables) do not, and in many (e.g. feeding an infant or buying a newspaper) language use is optional. The definitions of (both target and pedagogic) task and task type used by Long and Crookes, however, always focus on something that is done, not something that is said. Long defines (target) task using its everyday, non-technical meaning:

> a piece of work undertaken for oneself or for others, freely or for some reward. Thus, examples of tasks include painting a fence, dressing a child, filling out a form, buying a pair of shoes, making an airline reservation, borrowing a library book, taking a driving test, typing a letter, weighing a patient, sorting letters, taking a hotel reservation, writing a check, finding a street destination and helping someone across a road. In other words, by 'task' is meant the hundred and one things people *do* in everyday life, at work, at play, and in between. Tasks are the things people will tell you to do if you ask them and they are not applied linguists. (Long, 1985: 89)

Similarly, Crookes defines it as

> a piece of work or an activity, usually with a specified objective, undertaken as part of an educational course or at work. (Crookes, 1986: 1)

Task-based syllabuses utilizing such conceptions of task require a needs identification to be conducted in terms of the real-world *target tasks* learners are preparing to undertake — buying a train ticket, renting an apartment, reading a technical manual, solving a math problem, reporting a chemistry experiment, taking lecture notes, and so on — not in terms (say) of notions, functions, topics or situations. Bell (1981b: 159–70) describes a task-based needs identification of this sort for a canteen, or cafeteria, assistant (based on Boydell, 1970), as well as the way the resulting information can be used for diagnostic and syllabus design purposes. Swales (1990) offers examples and insightful discussion from the design of a university English for academic purposes program. Yalden (1987: 121–8) reports on the identification of the 'task types' relevant for a group of Canadian government officials who would be handling trade and commerce in embassies abroad. In addition, close to ready-made task-based needs analyses abound in the business world and in the public sector, e.g. in the *Dictionary of Occupational Titles* (US Department of Labor, 1977).

Valuable expertise in procedures for conducting such needs analyses was accumulated by ESP specialists in the 1970s and 1980s (see, for example, Jupp & Hodlin, 1975; Mackay, 1978; Selinker, 1979), and can still be drawn upon, even though many of the early ESP program designers were working within a notional–functional framework. Increasingly, ESP specialists have become more aware of the complexities of needs analysis and the limitations of a purely linguistic focus (Høedt, 1981; Berwick, 1989) and have called for an increased emphasis on 'process': 'we need to see students in action — what are they actually *doing*. And we need to observe target performers in action.' (Robinson, 1987: 37).

Selection of tasks for inclusion in a syllabus is determined by the results of the task-based needs analysis. Learners will only rarely work on the target tasks themselves, however, especially in the early stages. That would often be too difficult, inefficient in terms of class time, logistically impossible, and irrelevant for some learners in heterogeneous classes when students' future needs vary. Instead, target tasks are first classified into *task types*. To take a simple example, serving breakfast, serving lunch, serving dinner and serving snacks and refreshments, might be classified into 'serving food and beverages' in a course for trainee flight attendants.

Pedagogic tasks are then derived from the task types and sequenced to form the *task-based syllabus*. It is the pedagogic tasks that teachers and students actually work on in the classroom. They will be increasingly accurate approximations (according to criteria such as communicative success, semantic accuracy, pragmatic appropriacy, and even grammatical correctness) to the target tasks which motivated their inclusion. Since target tasks will usually be more complex than their related pedagogic tasks, increasingly accurate approximation will normally imply students addressing increasingly complex pedagogical tasks. Simplicity and complexity will not result from application of traditional linguistic grading criteria, however, but reside in some aspects of the tasks themselves. The number of steps involved, the number of solutions to a problem, the number of parties involved and the saliency of their distinguishing features, the location (or not) of the task in displaced time and space, and other aspects of the intellectual challenge a pedagogic task poses are some of the potential grading and sequencing criteria that have been proposed (for discussion, see Brown, 1986, 1989; Brown & Yule, 1983; Candlin, 1987; Crookes, 1986; Long, 1985, to appear; Robinson, 1990).

The grading and sequencing of pedagogic tasks also depend in part on which of various pedagogic options are selected to accompany their use. It is here that some of the materials for writer–teacher–student negotiation of *learning process* urged by Breen and Candlin can be built into TBLT, and here, too, that the findings of a number of lines of SL classroom research since the late 1970s are most helpful. Relevant issues investigated include the effects on student comprehension of elaboratively, or interactionally, modified spoken and written discourse (for review, see Parker & Chaudron, 1987), the effects on student production of certain types of teacher questions (e.g. Brock, 1986; Tollefson, 1988), the quality and quantity of language use in whole-class and small group formats (e.g. Doughty & Pica, 1986; Bygate, 1988; and for review, Long & Porter, 1985), and relationships between different pedagogic task types (one-way and two-way, planned and unplanned, open and closed) and negotiation work and interlanguage destabilization (e.g. Berwick, 1988; Crookes & Rulon, 1988; Pica, 1987a; Pica, Holliday, Lewis & Morgenthaler, 1989; Varonis & Gass, 1985; and for review, Crookes, 1986; Long, 1989; Nunan, 1989; Pica, 1987b).

Such task-based syllabuses would usually, although not exclusively, imply assessment of student learning by way of task-based criterion-referenced tests, whose focus is whether or not students can perform some task to a given criterion, not their ability to complete discrete-point grammar items. While beyond the scope of this chapter, suffice it to say that developments in criterion-referenced language testing since the late 1970s (see, for example Brown, 1989a, 1989b) hold great promise for language teaching in general and for TBLT in particular.

TBLT has potential, chiefly because of its compatibility with research findings on language learning, its principled approach to content selection, and its attempt to incorporate findings from classroom-centered research when making decisions concerning the design of materials and methodol-

ogy. It is not without problems of its own, however, of which the following
are some. There are no doubt others.

1. We have here sketched a psycholinguistic rationale for TBLT. Its
   research base is, as yet, limited, however, and some of the classroom
   research findings referred to may bear alternative interpretations, given
   the small scale and questionable methodology of some of the studies
   involved.
2. Given an adequate needs analysis, *selection* of tasks is relatively straightforward. Assessing task difficulty and *sequencing* pedagogic tasks is more
   of a problem. After reviewing a substantial body of SL work on sequencing, Schinnerer-Erben concluded:

   > [T]he criterion which are commonly used to establish traditional
   > sequences are rather feeble. Difficulty is not easily defined and it is
   > of questionable value. Frequency/utility is also difficult to establish
   > and has not been proven helpful in the learning process. And natural
   > sequences do not really exist in sufficient detail to be used as the
   > basis for a precise order, nor have they been shown to facilitate
   > learning in a second language situation. (Schinnerer-Erben, 1981:
   > 11)

   Little empirical support is yet available for the various proposed parameters of task difficulty, either, and little effort has been made even to
   define some of them operationally (but see Brown, 1989). Indeed, identification of valid, user-friendly sequencing criteria is one of the oldest
   unsolved problems in language teaching of all kinds (for useful discussion, see Widdowson, 1968: 134–44).
3. There is also the problem of finiteness, which afflicts all units we have discussed. How many tasks and task types are there? Where does one task
   end and the next begin? How many levels of analysis are needed? What
   hierarchical relationships exist between one level and another? For
   example, just as we criticized topic and situation for their vagueness and
   for the tendency for examples of each to overlap, so it must be recognized
   that task sometimes has the same problem. Some tasks, e.g. doing the
   shopping, either could or will involve others, e.g. catching a bus, paying
   a fare, choosing purchases, paying for purchases, and so on, and some of
   these 'sub-tasks' could easily be broken down still further, e.g. paying for
   purchases divided into counting money and checking change.
4. TBLT is relatively 'structured', in the sense of pre-planned and guided.
   While we have argued for this in terms of efficiency and relevance to
   students' needs, others could equally well object to the lesser degree of
   learner autonomy that the structuring admittedly produces. They could

claim that general learning processes need more protection than task relevance, and that if this is done, language learning will take care of itself.

5. While several classroom studies have been conducted of various issues in TBLT, no complete program that we know of has been implemented *and evaluated* which has fully adopted even the basic characteristics of TBLT sketched here, much less the detailed principles for making materials design and methodological decisions discussed elsewhere (Long, to appear). There are also few commercially published materials based on ideas of this sort, although (as described by White, 1988: 63–4) the BBC's (British Broadcasting Corporation) 'Get By In' series, e.g. *Get By In Italian* (BBC, 1981) appears to be relevant, as most certainly are some materials produced for an on-going 'content-based' program in Vancouver secondary schools (Early, Mohan & Hooper, 1989; Early, Thew & Wakefield, 1985; Mohan, 1986). A few programs have been reported which reflect some principles of TBLT (e.g. Yalden & Bosquet, 1984; Yalden, 1987; and see references in Breen, 1987), and some intellectually related small-scale efforts, accompanied by in-house materials development, are currently in various stages of implementation in Canada, Japan, the Philippines and Hawai'i. Not one of these innovations has been subjected to the kind of rigorous, controlled evaluation we think essential, however. We are therefore urging consideration of partly untested proposals.

Generic problems with analytic syllabuses

Advocates of process syllabuses, procedural syllabuses and TBLT differ in the psycholinguistic rational for their proposals, in the ways they define task, in whether they conduct a formal needs analysis to determine syllabus content, in how tasks are selected and sequenced, and in the methodological options, such as group work and a focus on form, that they prescribe and proscribe. Their proposals may well differ in other areas, too, but full, comparable statements are not available for all three proposals on some issues.

However, all three proposals have some areas of agreement: most fundamentally, their rejection of synthetic syllabuses and the units of analysis on which they are based, and their adoption of *task* as an alternative. Consequently, all share certain problems. A serious one is the difficulty of differentiating tasks, especially tasks and 'sub-tasks' nested within them, which in turn raises questions as to the finiteness of tasks (or task types), or their 'generative capacity'. Another problem is the issue of task difficulty, i.e. of determining the relevant grading and sequencing criteria. These are problems never resolved for synthetic syllabuses, either, of course, despite periodic discussion of such criteria as frequency, valency and (undefined and so unhelpful) 'difficulty', but that does not absolve users of tasks from doing better. Finally, none of the proposals has yet been subjected to a rigorous field evaluation, a situation which will be difficult to resolve as long as funding (at least in the US) continues to be allocated to 'training', but not research in language teaching.

Summary and Conclusion

Choice of the unit of analysis in syllabus design is crucial for all aspects of a language teaching program. A variety of units, including word, structure, notion, function, topic and situation, continue to be employed in synthetic syllabuses. While each is obviously relevant for linguistic analyses of a target language, none finds much support as a meaningful acquisition unit from a language learner's perspective. Task has more recently appeared as the unit of analysis in three analytic, Type B alternatives: procedural, process and task syllabuses. Each of these has certain limitations, too, but when combined with a focus on form, the task finds more support in SLA research as a viable acquisition unit. While still in need of controlled field testing, task-based language teaching shows some potential as an integrated approach to program design, implementation and evaluation.

Acknowledgments

We thank Chris Candlin, Kevin Gregg, Peter Robinson, Charlie Sato, and Dick Schmidt for detailed, often highly critical comments on an earlier version of this paper. We have incorporated those of their suggestions that would not have involved abandoning the whole enterprise. Errors that remain are very much our responsibility.

Notes

1. 'Method' appears here in inverted commas because there is good reason to believe that methods do not exist — at least, not where they would matter if they did, in the classroom. Classroom observational studies provide little evidence that supposedly different methods translate into different patterns of classroom language use by teachers and students, although it should be noted that all studies known to us to date have involved synthetic, Type A syllabuses, materials and methodology. This should come as no surprise, for several reasons. First, even as idealized by their creators, many methods overlap considerably in terms of prescribed and proscribed classroom practices. Second, any differences tend to become fuzzier as implemented in practice, especially over time. Third, research

consistently shows 'method' not to be a very salient construct for teachers, who, the same studies show, neither plan, nor implement, nor recall lessons in terms of methods, but as a series of activities or tasks. (For review of supporting literature, see Long, in press.)

2. Wilkins (1976: 2) classifies situational, notional and functional syllabuses as analytic. In a later section, we will try to show that, while this may be possible in theory, as implemented in practice, they have been synthetic.

3. Reflecting an apparent change of heart, the first and sixth (of ten) advantages claimed for notional–functional syllabuses by Finocchiaro & Brumfit (1983: 17) are that they 'set realistic learning tasks' and allow teachers 'to exploit sound psycholinguistic, sociolinguistic, linguistic and educational principles'.

4. Most people would agree that 'The last TESOL convention' is clearly a topic, for example, but even a brief conversation about it could quickly involve such matters as which of the speakers attended, travel to and from the site, the city and state it was held in, the Equal Rights Amendment, hotel arrangements, cost, professional acquaintances sighted, the publishers' exhibit, publishers' parties attended, publishers' commercial presentations, the job fair, possibly some reference to an academic presentation or two, and evaluative judgments about the whole 'fiesta'. Are these other topics, related topics, unrelated but co-occurring topics, sub-topics, the same 'general topic', or what? Further, would a different group of people discussing the same topic(s) cover the same ground?

5. See discussion above (under the heading of 'Structure') on the unlikelihood of synthetic SL learning.

6. Newmark & Reibel identified a psychological basis for their position in social learning theory (Bandura, 1977; Bandura & Walters, 1963; see Rosenthal & Zimmerman (1978) for its application to L1 acquisition). On the comparative inutility of instruction sequenced according to syntactic rule-based analysis of complexity, see Doughty (1991).

7. 70% is accepted as a satisfactory minimum passing grade on many criterion-referenced language tests, but higher cut-off points favor increased decision dependability for such tests. (See Brown (1989a, 1989b) for discussion of this and related issues.)

8. Possible exceptions arise when the learners are advanced, mature, and culturally or professionally accustomed to self-directed learning. See Allwright (1981) and Littlejohn (1985).

References

ALEXANDER, L. G. 1967, *First Things First.* London: Longman.

ALLWRIGHT, R. L. 1976, Language learning through communication practice. *ELT Documents* 76, 3, 2–14.

—— 1981, What do we want teaching materials for? *ELT Journal* 36, 1, 5–18.

ATKINSON, M. 1979, Prerequisites for reference. In E. OCHS and B. B. SCHIEFFELIN (eds) *Developmental Pragmatics* (pp. 229–49). New York: Academic Press.

AUERBACH, N. and BURGESS, D. 1985, The hidden curriculum of survival ESL. *TESOL Quarterly* 19, 3, 475–95.

AVRICH, P. 1980, *The Modern School Movement: Anarchism and Education in the United States.* Princetown, NJ: Princeton University Press.

BANDURA, A. 1977, *Social Learning Theory.* New York: General Learning Press.

BANDURA, A. and WALTERS, R. 1963, *Social Learning and Personality Development*. New York: Holt.

BBC 1981, *Get By In Italian*. London: British Broadcasting Corporation.

BELL, R. T. 1981a, Notional syllabuses: To grade or not to grade. In D. RICHARDS (ed.) *Communicative Course Design* (RELC Occasional Paper No. 17; pp. 14–24). Singapore: RELC.

—— 1981b, *An Introduction to Applied Linguistics. Approaches and Methods in Language Teaching*. London: Batsford.

BERETTA, A. 1986, Focus on the Bangalore classroom: An empirical study. Paper presented at the 20th annual TESOL convention, Anaheim, CA.

—— 1989, Attention to form or meaning? Error treatment in the Bangalore Project. *TESOL Quarterly* 23, 2, 283–303.

—— 1990, Implementation of the Bangalore Project. *Applied Linguistics* 11, 4, 321–37.

BERETTA, A. and DAVIES, A. 1985, Evaluation of the Bangalore project. *ELT Journal* 39, 2, 121–7.

BERWICK, R. F. 1988, The effect of task variation in teacher-led groups on repair of English as a foreign language. Unpublished doctoral dissertation. Vancouver, BC: University of British Columbia.

—— 1989, Needs assessment in language programming: From theory to practice. In R. K. JOHNSON (ed.) *The Second Language Curriculum* (pp. 48–62). Cambridge: Cambridge University Press.

BLEY-VROMAN, R. 1986, Hypothesis testing in second language acquisition theory. *Language Learning* 36, 3, 353–76.

BOWERMAN, M. 1982, Starting to talk worse: Clues to language acquisition from children's late speech errors. In S. STRAUSS (ed.) *U-shaped Behavioral Growth*. New York: Academic Press.

BOYDELL, T. H. 1970, *A Guide to Job Analysis*. London: Bacie.

BREEN, M. P. 1984, Process syllabuses for the language classroom. In C. J. BRUMFIT (ed.) *General English Syllabus Design. ELT Documents* 118, 47–60.

—— 1987a, Learner contributions to task design. In C. N. CANDLIN and D. MURPHY (eds) *Language Learning Tasks*. (Lancaster Practical Papers in English Language Education, Vol. 7, pp. 23–46). Englewood Cliffs, NJ: Prentice-Hall.

—— 1987b, Contemporary paradigms in syllabus design. Parts 1 & 2. *Language Teaching* 20, 2, 81–92; 3, 157–74.

BREEN, M. P. and CANDLIN, C. 1980, The essentials of a communicative curriculum in language teaching. *Applied Linguistics* 1, 2, 89–112.

BREEN, M. P., CANDLIN, C. N. and WATERS, A. 1979, Communicative materials design: Some basic principles. *RELC Journal* 10, 1–13.

BROCK, C. A. 1986, The effects of referential questions on ESL classroom discourse. *TESOL Quarterly* 20, 1, 47–59.

BROWN, G. 1986, Grading and professionalism in ELT. In P. MEARA (ed.) *Spoken Language* (British Studies in Applied Linguistics, 1; pp. 3–14). London: Centre for Information on Language Teaching.

—— 1989, Making sense: The interaction of linguistic expression and contextual information. *Applied Linguistics* 10, 1, 98–108.

BROWN, G. and YULE, G. 1983, *Teaching the Spoken Language*. Cambridge: Cambridge University Press.

BROWN, J. D. 1989a, Criterion-referenced test reliability. *University of Hawai'i Working Papers in ESL* 8, 1, 79–113.

—— 1989b, *Language Testing. A Practical Guide to Proficiency, Placement, Diagnostic and Achievement Testing*. MS. Honolulu, Hawai'i: Department of ESL, University of Hawai'i at Mānoa.

BRUMFIT, C. J. 1981, Notional syllabuses revisited: A response. *Applied Linguistics* 2, 1, 90–2.

—— 1984a, Function and structure of a state school syllabus for learners of second or foreign languages with heterogeneous needs. *ELT Documents* 118, 75–82.

—— 1984b, The Bangalore Procedural Syllabus. *ELT Journal* 38, 4, 233–41.

BYGATE, M. 1988, Units of oral expression and language learning in small group interaction. *Applied Linguistics* 9, 1, 59–82.

CANDLIN, C. N. 1972, Sociolinguistics and communicative language teaching. *ITL Review of Applied Linguistics* 16, 37–44.

—— 1976, Communicative language teaching and the debt to pragmatics. In C. RAMEH (ed.) *Semantics: Theory and Application* (Georgetown University Round Table on Languages and Linguistics, pp. 237–56). Washington, DC: Georgetown University Press.

—— 1984, Syllabus design as a critical process. *ELT Documents* 118, 29–46.

—— 1987, Towards task-based language learning. In C. N. CANDLIN and D. MURPHY (eds) *Language Learning Tasks* (Lancaster Practical Papers in English Language Education, Vol. 7, pp. 5–22). Englewood Cliffs, NJ: Prentice-Hall.

CANDLIN, C. N. and MURPHY, D. (eds) 1987, *Language Learning Tasks* (Lancaster Practical Papers in English Language Education, Vol. 7). Englewood Cliffs, NJ: Prentice-Hall.

CATHCART, R. L. 1989, Authentic discourse and the survival English curriculum. *TESOL Quarterly* 23, 1, 105–29.

CELCE-MURCIA, M. and HILLES, S. 1988, *Techniques and Resources in Teaching Grammar*. Oxford: Oxford University Press.

CHAUDRON, C. 1988, *Second Language Classrooms: Research on Teaching and Learning*. New York: Cambridge University Press.

Commonwealth Office of Education 1967, *Situational English* (parts 1–3). London: Longman.

COOK, V. J. 1971, Freedom and control in language teaching materials. In R. W. RUTHERFORD (ed.) *BAAL Seminar Papers 1970: Problems in the Preparation of Foreign Language Teaching Materials* (pp. 65–73). York: Child Language Survey.

—— 1974, *English Topics*. Oxford: Oxford University Press.

—— 1978, Some ways of organising language. *Audio-Visual Journal* 16, 2, 89–94.

—— 1985, Language functions, social factors, and second language learning and teaching. *International Review of Applied Linguistics* 23, 3, 177–98.

CORDER, S. P. 1967, The significance of learners' errors. *IRAL* 5, 161–70.

CREDIF 1961, *Voix et Images de France*. Paris: Didier.

CROMBIE, W. 1985, *Relational Syllabuses*. Oxford: Oxford University Press.

CROOKES, G. 1986, *Task Classification: A Cross-disciplinary Review* (Tech. Rep. No. 4). Honolulu: Center for Second Language Classroom Research, Social Science Research Institute, University of Hawai'i at Mānoa.

—— 1989, Planning and interlanguage variation. *Studies in Second Language Acquisition* 11, 4, 267–83.

—— 1991, Second language speech production research: A methodologically oriented review. *Studies in Second Language Acquisition* 13, 2, 113–32.

CROOKES, G. and LONG, M. H. 1987, Task-based second language teaching: A brief report. *Modern English Teacher* (Tokyo) 24, 5, 26–8, and 6, 20–3.

CROOKES, G. and RULON, K. A. 1988, Topic and feedback in native speaker/non-native speaker conversation. *TESOL Quarterly* 22, 4, 675–81.

CROSS, D. 1980. Personalized language learning. In H. B. ALTMAN and C. V. JAMES (eds) *Foreign Language Teaching: Meeting Individual Needs* (pp. 111–24). Oxford: Pergamon.

CRYSTAL, D. 1981, *Directions in Applied Linguistics.* London: Academic Press.

DAKIN, J. 1973, *The Language Laboratory and Modern Language Teaching.* London: Longman.

DOUGHTY, C. 1991, Second language instruction does make a difference: Evidence from an empirical study of second language relativization. *Studies in Second Language Acquisition* 13, 4, 431–70.

DOUGHTY, C. and PICA, T. 1986, 'Information gap' tasks: Do they facilitate second language acquisition? *TESOL Quarterly* 20, 2, 305–26.

EARLY, M., MOHAN, B. A. and HOOPER, H. R. 1989, The Vancouver School Board language and content project. In J. H. ESLING (ed.) *Multicultural Education and Policy: ESL in the 1990s* (pp. 107–21). Toronto: OISE.

EARLY, M., THEW, C. and WAKEFIELD, P. 1985, *ESL Across the Curriculum K-12.* Victoria, BC: Ministry of Education.

ECKERSLEY, C. E. 1938–42, *Essential English for Foreign Students* (vols 1–4). London: Longmans, Green.

ECKMAN. F., BELL, L. and NELSON, D. 1988, On the generalization of relative clause instruction in the acquisition of English as a second language. *Applied Linguistics* 9, 1, 1–20.

ELLIS, R. 1985, *Understanding Second Language Acquisition.* Oxford: Oxford University Press.

ERVIN-TRIPP, S. 1978, Some features of early child–adult dialogues. *Language in Society* 7, 257–73.

ETHERTON, A. R. B. 1979, The communicational syllabus in practice. Case study I: Malaysia. *The English Newsletter* (Hong Kong), 7, 2, 17–26.

FAUCETT, L., WEST, M., PALMER, H. and THORNDIKE, E. L. 1936, *The Interim Report on Vocabulary Selection for the Teaching of English as a Foreign Language.* London: P. S. King.

FERREIRA, L. 1981, *Notion by Notion.* Rowley, MA: Newbury House.

FINOCCHIARO, M. 1970, *Let's Talk.* New York: Regents.

FINOCCHIARO, M. and BRUMFIT, C. J. 1983, *The Functional Notional Approach.* Oxford: Oxford University Press.

FREIRE, P. 1970, *Pedagogy of the Oppressed.* Harmondsworth: Penguin.

—— 1972, *Cultural Action for Freedom.* Harmondsworth: Penguin.

GIVON, T. 1984. *Syntax: A Functional–Typological Introduction, Volume 1.* Amsterdam: John Benjamins.

GOODENOUGH, P. R. and WEINER, S. L. 1978, The role of conversational passing moves in the management of topical transitions. *Discourse Processes* 1, 395–404.

GREENWOOD, J. 1985, Bangalore revisited: A reluctant complaint. *ELT Journal* 39, 4, 268–73.

HALLIDAY, M. A. K., McINTOSH, A. and STREVENS, P. 1964, *The Linguistic Sciences and Language Teaching.* London: Longman.

HATCH, E. 1978, Discourse analysis and second language acquisition. In E. M. HATCH (ed.) *Second Language Acquisition* (pp. 401–35). Rowley, MA: Newbury House.

—— 1983, *Psycholinguistics: A Second Language Perspective*. Rowley, MA: Newbury House.

HIRSHON, S. with BUTLER, J. 1983, *And Also Teach Them to Read*. Westport, CT: Lawrence Hill.

HØEDT, J. 1981, The study of needs analysis. In J. HØEDT and R. TURNER (eds) *New Bearings in LSP* (pp. 77–89). Copenhagen: Copenhagen School of Economics.

HOLT, J. 1972. *Freedom and Beyond*. Harmondsworth: Penguin.

HOWATT, A. P. R. 1984, *A History of English Language Teaching*. Oxford: Oxford University Press.

HUEBNER, T. 1983, Linguistic systems and linguistic change in an interlanguage. *Studies in Second Language Acquisition* 6, 1, 33–53.

ILLICH, I, 1971, *Deschooling Society*. New York: Harper and Row.

JEFFERSON, G. 1978, Sequential aspects of storytelling in conversation. In J. SCHENKEIN (ed.) *Studies in the Organization of Conversation Interaction* (pp. 25–67). New York: Academic Press.

JONES, L. 1979, *Notions in English*. Cambridge: Cambridge University Press.

JUPP, T. C. and HODLIN, S. 1975, *Industrial English*. London: Heinemann.

KEENAN, E. OCHS 1974, Conversational competence in children. *Journal of Child Language* 1, 2, 163–85.

KELLERMAN, E. 1985, If at first you do succeed . . . In S. M. GASS and C. G. MADDEN (eds) *Input in Second Language Acquisition* (pp. 345–53). Rowley, MA: Newbury House.

KENNEDY, G. D. 1989, Collocations: Where grammar and vocabulary teaching meet. Paper presented at the RELC seminar, Singapore.

Kementerian Pelajaran Malaysia 1975, *English Language Syllabus in Malaysian Schools (Levels 4–5)*. Kuala Lumpar: Dewan Bahasa dan Pustaka, Kementerian Pelajaran.

KOURAOGO, P. 1987, EFL curriculum renewal and INSET in difficult circumstances. *ELT Journal* 41, 3, 171–8.

KRASHEN, S. D. 1982, *Principles and Practice in Second Language Acquisition*. Oxford: Pergamon.

—— 1985, *The Input Hypothesis*. London: Longman.

KRASHEN, S. D. and TERRELL, T. D. 1983, *The Natural Approach: Language Acquisition in the Classroom*. San Francisco, CA: The Alemany Press.

LARSEN-FREEMAN, D. and LONG, M. H. 1991, *An Introduction to Second Language Acquisition Research*. London: Longman.

LEVELT, W. J. M. 1978, Skill theory and second language teaching. *Studies in Second Language Acquisition* 1, 1, 53–70.

LIGHTBOWN, P. M. 1983, Exploring relationships between developmental and instructional sequences in L2 acquisition. In H. W. SELIGER and M. H. LONG (eds) *Classroom-oriented Research in Second Language Acquisition* (pp. 217–43). Rowley, MA: Newbury House.

LITTLEJOHN, A. 1985, Learner choice in language study. *ELT Journal* 39, 4, 253–61.

LONG, M. H. 1978, Review of *English in Physical Science*, J. P. B. Allen and H. G. Widdowson. *Language Learning* 28, 2, 443–55.

—— 1985, A role for instruction in second language acquisition: Task-based language teaching. In K. HYLTENSTAM and M. PIENEMANN (eds) *Modelling and Assessing Second Language Acquisition* (pp. 77–99). Clevedon: Multilingual Matters.

—— 1988, Instructed interlanguage development. In L. M. BEEBE (ed.) *Issues in*

Second Language Acquisition: Multiple Perspectives (pp. 115–41). New York: Harper and Row.
—— 1989, Task, group, and task-group interactions. *University of Hawai'i Working Papers in ESL* 8, 2, 1–26. Also in S. ARIVAN (ed.) *Language Teaching Methodology for the Nineties* (pp. 31–50). Singapore: SEAMEO Regional Language Centre, 1990.
—— in press, Focus on form: A design feature in language teaching methodology. In K. DE BOT, D, COSTE, R. GINSBERG and C. KRAMSCH (eds) *Foreign Language Research in Cross-cultural Perspective*. Amsterdam: John Benjamins.
—— to appear, *Task-Based Language Teaching*. Oxford: Basil Blackwell.
LONG, M. H. and CROOKES, G. 1987, Intervention points in second language classroom processes. In B. K. DAS (ed.) *Patterns in Classroom Interaction in Southeast Asia* (pp. 177–203). Singapore: Singapore University Press/RELC.
—— 1992, Three approaches to task based syllabus design. *TESOL Quarterly* 26, 1, 27–56.
LONG, M. H. and PORTER, P. A. 1985, Group work, interlanguage talk and second language acquisition. *TESOL Quarterly* 19, 2, 207–27.
MACDONALD, T. 1985, *Making a New People: Education in Revolutionary Cuba*. Vancouver: New Star.
MCINTOSH, A. 1965, Saying. *Review of English Literature* 6, 2, 9–20.
MACKAY, R. 1978, Identifying the nature of the learner's needs. In R. MACKAY and A. MOUNTFORD (eds) *English for Specific Purposes* (pp. 21–42). London: Longman.
MACKAY, R. and MOUNTFORD, A. (eds) 1978, *English for Specific Purposes*. London: Longman.
MACKEY, W. F. 1965, *Language Teaching Analysis*. London: Longman.
MCKAY, S. 1980, Towards an integrated syllabus. In K. CROFT (ed.) *Readings in English as a Second Language* (pp. 72–84). Boston, MA: Little, Brown.
MACNAMARA, J. 1973, Nurseries, streets and classrooms: Some comparisons and deductions. *Modern Language Journal* 57, 250–4.
MCLAUGHLIN, B. M. 1988, Restructuring. Paper presented at the ninth Second Language Research Forum. Honolulu, HI: University of Hawai'i at Mānoa.
MADDEN, C. and REINHART, S. 1987, *Pyramids: Structurally-based Tasks for ESL Learners*. Ann Arbor, MI: University of Michigan Press.
MEISEL, H., CLAHSEN, H. and PIENEMANN, M. 1981, On determining developmental stages in second language acquisition. *Studies in Second Language Acquisition* 3, 2, 109–35.
MOHAN, B. A. 1977, Toward a situational curriculum. In H. D. BROWN, C. YORIO and R. CRYMES (eds) *On TESOL '77* (pp. 250–7). Washington, DC: TESOL.
—— 1986, An integrated framework for language and content learning. In M. L. TICKOO (ed.) *Language in Learning* (pp. 53–68). Singapore: SEAMEO Regional Language Centre.
NEWMARK, L. 1964, Grammatical theory and the teaching of English as a foreign language. In D. F. HARRIS (ed.) *The 1963 Conference Papers of the English Language Section of The National Association for Foreign Student Affairs* (pp. 5–8). New York: National Association for Foreign Student Affairs.
—— 1966, How not to interfere with language learning. *International Journal of American Linguistics* 32, 1, 77–83.

—— 1971, A minimal language teaching program. In P. PIMSLEUR and T. QUINN (eds) *The Psychology of Second Language Learning* (pp. 11–18). Cambridge: Cambridge University Press.

NEWMARK, L. and REIBEL, D. A. 1968, Necessity and sufficiency in language learning. *International Review of Applied Linguistics* 6, 145–64.

NUNAN, D. 1989, *Designing Tasks for the Communicative Classroom*. Cambridge: Cambridge University Press.

OGDEN, C. K. 1930, *Basic English: An Introduction with Rules and Grammar*. London: Kegan Paul, Trench & Trubner.

PARKER, K. and CHAUDRON, C. 1987, The effects of linguistic simplification and elaborative modifications in L2 comprehension. *University of Hawai'i Working Papers in ESL* 6, 2, 107–33.

PAULSTON, C. B. 1981, Notional syllabuses revisited: Some comments. *Applied Linguistics* 2, 1, 93–5.

PEARSON, E. 1983, Agreement and disagreement: A study of speech acts in discourse and ESL/EFL materials. MA thesis, Department of ESL, University of Hawai'i at Mānoa.

PICA, T. 1987a, Interlanguage adjustments as an outcome on NS–NNS negotiated interaction. *Language Learning* 37, 4, 563–93.

—— 1987b, Second language acquisition, social interaction, and the classroom. *Applied Linguistics* 8, 1, 1–25.

PICA, T., HOLLIDAY, L., LEWIS, N. and MORGENTHALER, L. 1989, Comprehensible output as an outcome of linguistic demands on the learner. *Studies in Second Language Acquisition* 11, 1, 63–90.

PIENEMANN, M. 1984, Psychological constraints on the teachability and learnability of languages. *Studies in Second Language Acquisition* 6, 186–214.

—— 1987, Psychological constraints on the teachability of languages. In C. PFAFF (ed.) *First and Second Language Acquisition Processes* (pp. 143–68). Rowley, MA: Newbury House.

PIENEMANN, M. and JOHNSTON, M. 1987, Factors influencing the development of language proficiency. In D. NUNAN (ed.) *Applying Second Language Acquisition Research* (pp. 45–141). Adelaide: National Curriculum Resource Centre.

PRABHU, N. S. 1980, Reactions and predictions. *Regional Institute of English South India Bulletin* 4, 1, 1–20.

—— 1984, Procedural syllabuses. In T. E. READ, (ed.) *Trends in Language Syllabus Design* (pp. 272–80). Singapore: Singapore University Press/RELC.

—— 1987, *Second Language Pedagogy*. Oxford: Oxford University Press.

—— 1990a, Comments on Alan Beretta's paper: 'Implementation of the Bangalore Project'. *Applied Linguistics* 11, 4, 338–40.

—— 1990b, Comments on Alan Beretta's paper: 'Attention to form or meaning? Error treatment in the Bangalore Project'. *TESOL Quarterly* 24, 1, 112–15.

RAMANI, E. 1987, Theorizing from the classroom. *English Language Teaching Journal* 41, 1, 3–11.

REIBEL, D. A. 1969, Language learning analysis. *International Review of Applied Linguistics* 7, 4, 283–94.

RICHARDS, J. C. 1984a, The secret life of methods. *TESOL Quarterly* 18, 1, 7–23.

—— 1984b, Language curriculum development. *RELC Journal* 15, 1, 1–29.

ROBINSON, Pauline 1987, Needs analysis: From product to process. In A.-M. CORNU, J. VANPARIJS, M. DELAHAYE and L. BATEN (eds) *Beads or Bracelet? How do we Approach LSP?* (Selected papers from the Fifth European

Symposium on LSP; pp. 32–44). Language Teaching Institute, Catholic University of Leuven, Belgium/Oxford University Press.

ROBINSON, Peter 1990, Task complexity and second language narrative discourse. Term paper, ESL 730 (Task-based language teaching). University of Hawai'i at Mānoa.

RODGERS, T. 1979, The Malaysian Communicative Syllabus: A developer's reflections. *The English Newsletter* (Hong Kong), 7, 3, 19–25.

—— 1984, Communicative syllabus design and implementation: Reflection on a decade of experience. In J. A. S. READ (ed.) *Trends in Language Syllabus Design*. Singapore University Press.

ROSENTHAL, T. L. and ZIMMERMAN, B. J. 1978, *Social Learning and Cognition*. New York: Academic Press.

SAMAH, A. A. 1984, The English language (communicational) curriculum for upper secondary schools in Malaysia: Rationale, design and implementation. In J. A. S. READ (ed.) *Trends in Language Syllabus Design*. Singapore: Singapore University Press.

SATO, C. J. 1986, Conversation and interlanguage development: Rethinking the connection. In R. R. DAY (ed.) *Talking to Learn: Conversation in Second Language Acquisition* (pp. 23–45). Rowley, MA: Newbury House.

SCHINNERER-ERBEN, J. 1981, Sequencing redefined. *Practical Papers in English Language Education* (University of Lancaster, UK), 4, 1–29.

SCHMIDT, R. W. 1990, The role of consciousness in second language learning. *Applied Linguistics* 11, 2, 17–46.

—— 1993, Consciousness, learning, and interlanguage pragmatics. In G. KASPER and S. BLUM-KULKA (eds) *Interlanguage Pragmatics*. Oxford: Oxford University Press.

SCHMIDT, R. W. and FROTA, S. N. 1986, Developing basic conversational ability in a second language: A case study of an adult learner of Portuguese. In R. R. DAY (ed.) *Talking to Learn: Conversation in Second Language Acquisition* (pp. 237–326). Rowley, MA: Newbury House.

SCHUMANN, J. 1979, The acquisition of English negation by speakers of Spanish: A review of the literature. In R. ANDERSEN (ed.) *The Acquisition and Use of Spanish and English as a First and Second Language* (pp. 3–32). Washington, DC: TESOL.

SCOLLON, R. 1973, A real early stage: An unzipped condensation of a dissertation on child language. *University of Hawai'i Working Papers in Linguistics* 5, 6, 67–81.

SELINKER, L. 1979, The use of specialist informants in discourse analysis. *International Review of Applied Linguistics* 17, 2, 189–215.

SELINKER, L., TARONE, E. and HANZELI, V. 1981, *English for Academic and Technical Purposes*. Rowley, MA: Newbury House.

SINCLAIR, J. McH. 1987, Collocation: A progress report. In R. STEELE and T. THREADGOLD (eds) *Language Topics: Essays in Honor of Michael Halliday* (pp. 319–31). Philadelphia, PA: John Benjamins.

SINCLAIR, J. McH. and RENOUF, A. 1988, A lexical syllabus for language learning. In R. CARTER and M. MCCARTHY (eds) *Vocabulary and Language Teaching* (pp. 140–58). New York: Longman.

SIROIS, P. and DORVAL, B. 1988, The role of returns to a prior topic in the negotiation of topic change: A developmental investigation. *Journal of Psycholinguistic Research* 17, 3, 185–210.

SPRING, J. 1975, *A Primer of Libertarian Education*. Montreal: Black Rose Books.

STENHOUSE, M. 1975, *An Introduction to Curriculum Research and Development*. London: Heinemann.

STERN, H. H. 1983, Toward a multidimensional foreign language curriculum. In R. G. MEAD (ed.) *Foreign Languages: Key Links in the Chain of Learning* (pp. 120–44). Middlebury, VT: NE Conference on the Teaching of Foreign Languages.

SWAIN, M. 1985, Communicative competence: Some roles of comprehensible input and comprehensible output in its development. In S. M. GASS and C. G. MADDEN (eds) *Input in Second Language Acquisition* (pp. 235–53). Rowley, MA: Newbury House.

SWALES, J. 1985, *Episodes in ESP*. Hemel Hempstead, UK: Prentice-Hall.

—— 1990, *Genre Analysis: English in Academic and Research Settings*. Cambridge: Cambridge University Press.

TICKOO, M. (ed.) 1988, *ESP: State of the Art*. Singapore: Singapore University Press/RELC.

TOLLEFSON, J. W. 1988, Measuring communication in ESL/EFL classes. *Cross Currents* 15, 1, 37–46.

ULLMAN, R. 1982, A broadened curriculum framework for second languages. *ELT Journal* 36, 4, 255–62.

US Department of Labor 1977, *Dictionary of Occupational Titles* (2nd edn). Washington, DC: Department of Labor.

VAN OOSTEN, J. 1984, A unified view of topic. In Berkeley Linguistics Society *Proceedings of the 10th Annual Meeting of the Berkeley Linguistic Society* (pp. 372–85). Berkeley, CA: Berkeley Linguistic Society.

VARONIS, E. M. and GASS, S. M. 1985, Non-native/non-native conversations: A model for negotiation of meaning. *Applied Linguistics* 6, 1, 71–90.

VENTOLA, E. 1987, Textbook dialogues and discourse realities. In W. LORSCHER and R. SCHULTZE (eds) *Perspectives on Language in Performance* (pp. 399–411). Tubingen: Gunter Narr.

VILAS, C. M. 1986, *The Sandinista Revolution. National Liberation and Social Transformation in Central America*. New York: Monthly Review Press.

WELFORD, A. R. 1968, *Fundamentals of Skill*. London: Methuen.

WEST, M. 1926, *Bilingualism (With Special Reference to Bengal)*. Calcutta: Bureau of Education, India.

WHITE, L. 1987, Against comprehensible input: The input hypothesis and the development of L2 competence. *Applied Linguistics* 8, 1, 95–110.

—— 1989, The principle of adjacency in second language acquisition: Do learners observe the subset principle? In S. M. GASS and J. SCHACHTER (eds) *Linguistic Perspective on Second Language Acquisition* (pp. 134–58). Cambridge: Cambridge University Press.

WHITE, R. V. 1988, *The ELT Curriculum. Design, Innovation and Management*. Oxford: Basil Blackwell.

WIDDOWSON, H. G. 1968, The teaching of English through science. In J. DAKIN, B. TIFFEN and H. G. WIDDOWSON. *Language in Education: The Problem in Commonwealth Africa and the Indo-Pakistan Sub-continent* (pp. 115–75). London: Oxford University Press.

—— 1971, The teaching of rhetoric to students of science and technology. *Science and Technology in a Second Language*, 7. Reprinted in *Explorations in Applied Linguistics* (1979, pp. 7–17). Oxford: Oxford University Press.

54 TASKS IN A PEDAGOGICAL CONTEXT

—— 1978, Notional–functional syllabuses: 1978, part 4. In C. H. BLATCHFORD and J. SCHACHTER (eds) *On TESOL '78* (pp. 32–5). Washington, DC: TESOL.

—— 1979, *Explorations in Applied Linguistics*. Oxford: Oxford University Press.

WILKINS, D. A. 1972, Grammatical, situational and notional syllabuses. In Association Internationale de Linguistique Appliquée (ed.) *Proceedings of the 3rd International Congress of Applied Linguistics*. Heidelberg: Julius Groose Verlag. Reprinted in C. J. BRUMFIT and K. JOHNSON (eds) *The Communicative Approach to Teaching* (1979, pp. 82–90). Oxford: Oxford University Press.

—— 1974, Notional syllabuses and the concept of a minimum adequate grammar. In S. P. CORDER and E. ROULET (eds) *Linguistic Insights in Applied Linguistics*. AIMAV/Didier.

—— 1976, *Notional Syllabuses*. Oxford: Oxford University Press.

—— 1981, Notional syllabuses revisited. *Applied Linguistics* 2, 1, 83–90.

WILLIAMS, M. 1988, Language taught for meetings and language used in meetings: Is there anything in common? *Applied Linguistics* 9, 1, 45–58.

WILLIS, D. and WILLIS, J. 1988, *Collins COBUILD English Course*. London: Collins.

YALDEN, J. 1983, *The Communicative Syllabus: Evolution, Design, and Implementation*. Oxford: Pergamon.

—— 1987, *Principles of Course Design for Language Teaching*. Cambridge: Cambridge University Press.

YALDEN, J. and BOSQUET, M. 1984, Analysis and description of communication needs and design of prototypes for the preparation of language specific pedagogic materials. Report prepared for the Department of External Affairs, Government of Canada, Centre for Applied Language Studies, Carleton University, Ottawa.

ZOBL, H. 1985, Grammars in search of input and intake. In S. M. GASS and C. G. MADDEN (eds) *Input in Second Language Acquisition* (pp. 329–44). Rowley, MA: Newbury House.

2 Task-based Syllabus Design: Selecting, Grading and Sequencing Tasks

DAVID NUNAN
National Centre for English Language Teaching Research,
Macquarie University

Introduction

The purpose of this chapter is to articulate some of the concerns and problems confronting those wishing to incorporate 'task' as a central element in syllabus planning and development. Within the field of language curriculum design, a traditional distinction is drawn between syllabus design and methodology. The former is concerned with the selection, justification and sequencing of linguistic and experiential content, while the latter is concerned with the selection, justification and sequencing of learning tasks and activities. However, with the development of communicative approaches to language teaching, this distinction has become difficult to sustain, as the 'what' and 'how' of the curriculum begin to merge (see, for example, Breen, 1984).

Incorporation of 'task' as a basic element in the design phase of the curriculum has created significant problems for grading and sequencing because of the number of factors involved, and the interaction between these factors. While a healthy research agenda has developed in recent years, the conceptual and empirical thrust of this research has been methodological in flavor, focusing on psycholinguistically motivated rationales for selecting and sequencing tasks. The dilemma for the syllabus designer, however, is on selecting and sequencing tasks which are not only psycholinguistically motivated, but which are also related in some principled fashion to the things which the learner might actually or potentially wish to do outside the classroom (see, for example, Long & Crookes, Chapter 1, this volume). The essential problem to be solved, then, is how to achieve a rational articulation in selecting, sequencing and integrating tasks so that the curriculum is more than an untidy 'rag-bag' of tasks which, while theoretically motivated in psycholinguistic terms, are unrelated to each other and disconnected from the learner.

In this chapter, I shall first provide a context for addressing this central problem by looking at the scope and changing nature of syllabus design. I shall also outline a framework for analysing tasks. The framework can be used to catalogue and summarize the task research agenda as it has emerged thus far. Finally, I shall present a planning grid for use in task-based syllabus design, a grid which can facilitate the process of developing principled links between the target tasks which learners need to perform beyond the class-room, but which also incorporates what is known about 'good' language learning tasks.

The Scope and Changing Nature of Syllabus Design

In recent years, considerable attention has been paid to the scope of syllabus design. Within the literature, two perspectives emerge. The first of these, the traditional or conservative view, sees syllabus design in a rather restricted light. Allen (1984: 61), for instance, asserts that syllabus design '. . . refers to that sub-part of curriculum which is concerned with a specification of what units will be taught (as distinct from how they will be taught to, which is a matter for methodology).'

However, with the development of communicative approaches to language teaching, it has become apparent that this traditional distinction is becoming increasingly difficult to sustain. Breen (1984) highlights the dilemma but points out that embracing communicative views of language learning and teaching forces us to consider both the destination and the route of learning, that we learn to communicate by communicating. Communicative language learning and teaching has forced a radical rethinking of key curriculum questions. These questions relate to the traditional domains of syllabus design (what?, why? and when?), methodology (how?), and assessment (how well?).

Answering the 'what' and 'why' questions requires the syllabus designer to justify input. When syllabuses are defined largely in terms of linguistic content, the answer is usually in linguistic terms. However, when content is defined in terms of communicative tasks of one sort or another, the answers are more likely to be made with reference to the learner or with reference to psycholinguistic processes of acquisition. Answering 'what' and 'why' questions with reference to the learner leads us towards needs analysis and the specification of target language performance and will result in a methodology predicated on learning as rehearsal. In other words, class time will be largely devoted to tasks in which learners rehearse those communicative behaviors which they wish or need to carry out outside the classroom. A psycholinguistic rationale will result in classroom tasks which attempt to replicate those conditions which, it is hypothesized, will facilitate as yet little understood psycholinguistic processes of acquisition. (It could be argued that a comprehensive curriculum would fulfil both pragmatic and psycholinguistic conditions along the lines suggested, for example, by Long, 1985.) For a detailed discussion on the various points of departure for syllabus design, see Nunan (1988a, 1989).

The changing scope and nature of curriculum development brought about by communicative views of language learning and teaching are illustrated in Figure 1.

TRADITIONAL   COMMUNICATIVE
                          NEEDS ANALYSIS
Identify current proficiency   Obtain information about
level   proficiency, learners' goals,
                                                     preferences, etc.

                          GROUPING LEARNERS
Group learners according to   Group learners according
proficiency level   to proficiency, goals,
                                                     learning style, etc.

                          CONTENT SELECTION
Select and sequence   Derive content from
grammar, pronunciation   input data and tasks
and vocabulary

                          TASK SELECTION
Select with reference to   Select with reference to
content and theory of   learners' goals, theory
learning   of learning and learner
                                                     preferences

                          ASSESSMENT
Assess mastery of linguistic   Assess achievement of
content   communicative goals

FIGURE 1   *'Traditional' and communicative curriculum models compared*

From Figure 1, it can be seen that the development of communicative approaches to language teaching has had a major impact on curriculum processes as well as outcomes. In the first place, much more information about and, desirably, from learners needs to be taken into consideration. Secondly, it is worth noting the priority of tasks over linguistic content (that is, grammar, lexis and phonology). In the traditional model, classroom tasks and exercises are selected with reference to the prior selection of linguistic content. With communicative models, tasks are selected first, and the linguistic elements are selected with reference to these.

There is, as has already been mentioned, a growing body of research which can assist the syllabus designer to make informed decisions relating to the selection and grading of tasks on psycholinguistic grounds. This research can be summarized using the framework for analyzing tasks which is set out in the following section.

A Framework for Analysing Tasks

If we look in the literature, we shall see that task is variously defined. Here are some examples:

Long suggests that a task is:

> . . . a piece of work undertaken for oneself or for others, freely or for some reward. Thus, examples of tasks include painting a fence, dressing a child, filling out a form, buying a pair of shoes, making an airline reservation, borrowing a library book, taking a driving test, typing a letter, weighing a patient, sorting letters, taking a hotel reservation, writing a cheque, finding a street destination and helping someone across a road. In other words, by 'task' is meant the hundred and one things people do in everyday life, at work, at play, and in between. (Long, 1985: 89)

This is a non-pedagogical definition in that it describes the sorts of things individuals do with language outside the classroom, and is the sort of characterization which might be offered by a learner if asked why he/she is learning the language. From a language teaching perspective, it is worth noting that some of the tasks need not necessarily involve the use of language. There is also the problem of knowing where one task ends and another begins. (I should point out that this is a problem shared by all approaches to task-based learning.)

Richards, Platt & Weber offer a more pedagogically oriented definition. They suggest that a task is:

an activity or action which is carried out as the result of processing or understanding language (i.e. as a response). For example, drawing a map while listening to a tape, listening to an instruction and performing a command, may be referred to as tasks. Tasks may or may not involve the production of language. A task usually requires the teacher to specify what will be regarded as successful completion of the task. The use of a variety of different kinds of tasks in language teaching is said to make teaching more communicative . . . since it provides a purpose for a classroom activity which goes beyond the practice of language for its own sake. (Richards, Platt & Weber, 1985: 289)

Despite their differences, these definitions have a common characteristic; they both suggest that tasks are concerned with communicative language. In other words, they refer to undertakings in which learners comprehend, produce and interact in the target language in contexts in which they are focused on meaning rather than form. Following these characterizations, I shall define the communicative task as a piece of classroom work which involves learners in comprehending, manipulating, producing or interacting in the target language while their attention is principally focused on meaning rather than form. The task should also have a sense of completeness, being able to stand alone as a communicative act in its own right. The notion of 'completeness' is admittedly rather problematic, representing a continuum rather than a polar opposite. Additionally, when tasks are implemented in the classroom an observer's or participant's judgment will determine the degree of completeness as much as the characteristics of the task itself.

Minimally, a task will consist of some input data and one or more related activities or procedures. Input refers to the data that learners are to work on: it may be linguistic (e.g. a radio broadcast), non-linguistic (e.g. a set of photographs), or 'hybrid' (e.g. a road map). In addition, tasks will have, either explicitly or implicitly (and in most cases these are implicit) goals, roles of teachers and learners and a setting. This relatively simple scheme provides a useful framework for summarizing research on tasks.

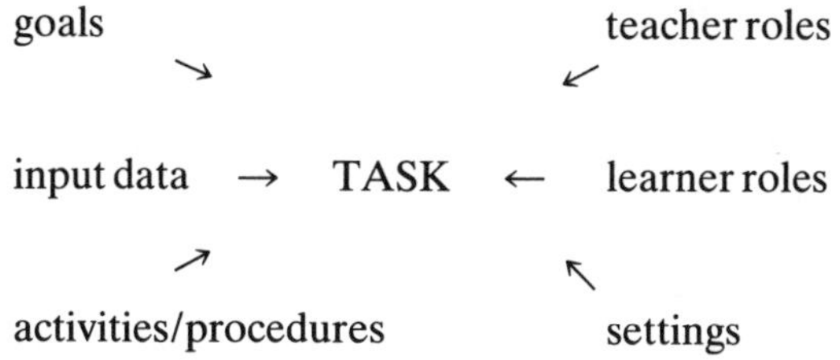

```
     goals                    teacher roles
              ↘            ↙

  input data  →   TASK   ←   learner roles

          ↗                ↖
  activities/procedures      settings
```

FIGURE 2   *Key components of tasks*

Research on Tasks

As we have already seen, major tasks for curriculum designers include the selection, grading and sequencing of linguistic content and pedagogic tasks. Initial selection is carried out with reference to the target goals of the learners and also with reference to theories of learning. Grading and sequencing are carried out with reference to priority of learner needs and also with reference to notions of difficulty. Determining difficulty is a major problem because of the number of factors involved (factors relating to any of the task elements as set out in Figure 1 may have an impact on difficulty). In addition, these factors interact. Some of the relevant research on task difficulty is set out in Table 1.

TABLE 1   *Task research on relevance to syllabus design*

Goals:
Brindley (1984): goals which reflect the communicative needs of learners have greater face validity.

Input data:
Porter & Roberts (1981): Aural texts written specifically for English language teaching differ significantly in their linguistic characteristics from genuine spoken discourse.
Brown & Yule (1983): The difficulty of listening texts is determined by: (a) the number of elements and the ease/difficulty of distinguishing between them and (b) text genre: descriptions are easier than instructions which are easier than stories which are easier than arguments or opinion-expressing texts.
Nunan (1985): Content familiarity is more significant than grammatical complexity in determining the difficulty of reading texts.
Morris & Stewart-Dore (1984): Input texts from different subject areas have their own distinctive generic structure.
Anderson & Lynch (1988): The difficulty of listening texts is determined by: information organization; familiarity of topic; explicitness and sufficiency of information; referring expressions (e.g. for young children pronominal referents are more difficult than full NP referents); text type.

Activities:
Long (1981): Two-way tasks prompt significantly more conversational adjustments than one-way tasks.
Brown & Yule (1983): The length of the speaking turn is a factor in the difficulty of speaking tasks.
Willing (1988): Learners' activity preferences can vary markedly, and are determined by cognitive style and personality variables.

TABLE 1 *Continued*

Brock (1986): Use of referential questions prompts significantly longer and more syntactically complex responses containing more connectives.

Doughty & Pica (1986): Required information exchange tasks generate significantly more interactional modifications than optional information exchange tasks.

Duff (1986): Convergent (e.g. problem solving) tasks produce more negotiation of meaning than divergent (e.g. debating) tasks.

Long & Crookes (1986): Use of referential questions results in greater mastery of experiential content.

Nunan (1987): Use of referential questions prompts more negotiation of meaning and syntactically and discoursally more complex language.

Nunan (1988b; 1988c): There are often dramatic mismatches between the activity preferences of teachers and students.

Prabhu (1987): Difficulty is determined by the amount and type of information provided, the number of steps of cognitive operations, the degree of precision called for, learners' knowledge of the world and the degree of abstractness (e.g. working with concepts is more difficult than working with objects or actions).

Roles:

Bruton & Samuda (1980): Learners are capable of correcting each other successfully.

Porter (1983): Learners produce more talk with other learners than with native speaking partners.

Porter (1983): Learners do not produce more errors when speaking with other learners.

Varonis & Gass (1985): Most negotiation of meaning occurs when learners are from different language backgrounds and different proficiency levels.

Wright (1987): There are two dimensions to learners' roles when carrying out classroom tasks: task-related activity or interactivity and interpersonal activity or interpersonality.

Settings:

Long, Adams, McLean & Castañas (1976): Small group tasks prompt students to use a greater range of language functions than teacher-fronted tasks.

Montgomery & Eisenstein (1985): Community-based learning experiences resulted in significantly increased language gains (including mastery of grammar) than classroom-based learning.

Doughty & Pica (1986): Small group tasks generate significantly more interactional modifications than teacher-fronted tasks.

Anderson & Boyle cited in Anderson & Lynch (1988): Success on listening tasks is significantly better when done in small groups than individually.

This summary of relevant research is illustrative rather than exhaustive. It serves to demonstrate the extensive body of literature to which syllabus designers can refer in selecting and sequencing tasks.

A Pedagogical Rationale for Selecting Tasks

As already indicated, the selection of tasks can proceed either with reference to the sorts of things learners will need to do outside the classroom, or with reference to either theoretical or empirical notions of what makes learners tick. The utilitarian dimension to task selection is sometimes overlooked, and there seems to be an assumption that learning takes place in a social and pragmatic vacuum. The distinction between utilitarian and psycholinguistic rationales for task selection is schematized in Figure 3, from Nunan (1989: 40).

Communicative classroom tasks

Task type	Real-world	Pedagogic
	↓	↓
Rationale	Rehearsal	Psycholinguistic
	↓	↓
Reference	Needs analysis	SLA theory/research

FIGURE 3   *Task selection: rationale and point of reference*

Tasks with a real-world rationale require learners to approximate, in class, the sorts of tasks required of them in the world beyond the classroom. (The term 'real-world' is used here as a form of shorthand. It is not suggested that the classroom is not 'real'.) Tasks with a pedagogic rationale, on the other hand, require learners to do things which it is extremely unlikely they would be called upon to do outside the classroom . . . while the selection of real-world tasks (as we shall call tasks with a real-world rationale) will proceed with reference to some form of needs analysis, pedagogic tasks will be selected with reference to some theory or model of second language acquisition. (Nunan, 1989: 40–1)

Dispute over the relative merits of needs driven and SLA driven tasks has found expression in the literature, as is evidenced in the following quotes:

Classroom activities should parallel the 'real world' as closely as possible. Since language is a tool of communication, methods and materials should concentrate on the message, not the medium. (Clarke & Silberstein, 1977: 51)

. . . what is wanted is a methodology which will . . . provide for communicative competence by functional investment. [Such a methodology] would engage the learners in problem-solving tasks as purposeful activities but without the rehearsal requirement that they should be realistic or 'authentic' as natural social behaviour. (Widdowson, 1987: 71)

Long (1985: 89) comes out strongly in favor of referencing tasks against the real world. He proposes the following four stage procedure in developing language programs:

1. identifying learners' needs,
2. defining syllabus content,
3. organizing language acquisition opportunities,
4. measuring student achievement.

He goes on to say that, 'If "task" will serve in all these capacities, it should provide the basis for naturally compatible decisions at all stages in programme design and implementation'. (See also Long & Crookes, Chapter 1 this volume.)

At the present time, what is needed is a means whereby the notions of rehearsal and functional investment (see Widdowson, 1987) might be brought together. Desirably, tasks should (1) be systematically linked to the things learners need to do in the real world, (2) incorporate what we know about the nature of successful communication, and (3) embody what we know about second language acquisition.

Bygate (1987) outlines one way in which this might be achieved. He suggests that oral interactions can be characterized in terms of routines. Routines are conventional (and therefore predictable) ways of presenting information which can focus on either information or interaction. Information routines contain frequently recurring types of information structures. These can be either expository (e.g. narration, description, instruction, comparison) or evaluative (e.g. explanation, justification, predication, decision). Interaction routines can be either service (e.g. a job interview) or social (e.g. a dinner party). A further feature of oral interaction is that the participants need constantly to negotiate meaning, and generally manage the interaction in terms of who is to say what, to whom, when and about what.

TABLE 2 *A framework for integrating pedagogic and psycholinguistic perspectives* (after Bygate, 1987)

| | Information | | Negotiation of meaning |
	Expository	Evaluative	Management of interaction
	narrate describe instruct compare	explain justify predict decide	
Interaction			
Service	job interview		
	booking a restaurant		
	buying stamps		
	enrolling in school		
	etc.		
Social	dinner party		
	coffee break		
	theatre queue		
	etc.		

Of course, life does not proceed through sets of finite interactional routines. Any interaction may, in fact, contain elements of any or all of the various elements identified by Bygate. That is, any encounter will contain informational and interactional elements as well as the negotiation of meaning and management of interaction. An alternative representation of Bygate's scheme is set out in Table 2. Such a table could be used to provide a map or profile of a given interaction.

Frameworks such as these provide the syllabus designer with a way of integrating learners' real-world or target communicative needs with the sorts of rhetorical macrofunctions or genres (e.g. narratives, descriptions, instructions) which have been proposed by systemic functional linguists (Halliday, 1985). Systemics also provides a social perspective on interaction, and a number of researchers are now beginning to incorporate insights from systemics into their work on tasks. I cite as an example Berwick (1988; Chapter 4 this volume) who found that genre was a significant factor in the generation of negotiation and repair.

A major challenge, and point of controversy concerns the relationship between form and function. Systemic-functionalists argue that function determines form (see, for example, Halliday, 1985; Martin 1985). According to Halliday:

> Every text — that is, everything that is said or written — unfolds in some context of use; furthermore, it is the uses of language that, over tens of thousands of generations, have shaped the system. Language has evolved to satisfy human needs; and the way it is organised is functional with respect to those needs — it is not arbitrary. A functional grammar is essentially a 'natural' grammar, in the sense that everything in it can be explained, ultimately, by reference to how language is used. (Halliday, 1985: xiii)

The opposite view is put by writers such as Gregg, who argues that:

> . . . one can understand form independent of function; however function is not enough to understand form. When Kumpf (1984), for instance, asserts that 'any grammatical form appears to fill a function in the discourse: it is the discourse context which creates the conditions under which the forms appear, and in order to explain the forms, it is necessary to refer to this context', she is making a claim that is far too strong to be tenable. What for instance is the discourse function of grammatical gender, or third person singular -s, vowel harmony? (Gregg, 1989: 26)

Gregg also points out that such arguments confuse competence and performance, that context explains the appearance of a form but not its existence.

The claims made by systemic-functionalists on the relationship between genre and linguistic form would seem to be eminently amenable to empirical investigation. To exemplify: one such claim is that a report will require the use of generic referents, simple present, lack of temporal sequence, and use of 'being' and 'having' processes. If reports were to appear which were not realized through such linguistic forms, but which were nonetheless effective and recognizable as reports, the approach (I refrain from using the term 'theory') would be seriously undermined. However, even if such an eventuality were to occur, the weaker, probabalistic claim that in general 'reports' will be characterized by the aforesaid forms, but will not be determined by them, may still provide useful guidance to the syllabus developer who is concerned with the practical issues of design rather than the theoretical ones of model-building.

Conclusion

In this chapter I have attempted to articulate some of the issues and concerns confronting those of us attempting to activate a task-based syllabus. I have argued that communicative views of language learning and teaching as well as a growing body of SLA research have significantly enhanced the status of 'task' as an important building block within the curriculum. Such activation, however, must proceed with reference to the key curriculum questions of selection, grading and sequencing. In this regard, the vast majority of available research has concerned itself with a psycholinguistically motivated rationale for selecting and sequencing tasks. However, the syllabus designer also requires a real-world rationale which allows tasks to be related in principled ways to the things which learners wish to do outside the classroom. In conclusion, it must be pointed out that for the first time syllabus designers are offered a substantial body of empirical data to draw on in formulating their programs, and the prospect is beginning to emerge that syllabus design itself might become a more equitable blend of science and art.

References

ALLEN, J. P. B. 1984, General purpose language teaching: A variable focus approach. In C. J. BRUMFIT (ed.) *General English Syllabus Design*. Oxford: Pergamon.
ANDERSON, A. and LYNCH, T. 1988, *Listening*. Oxford: Oxford University Press.
BERWICK, R. 1988, The effect of task variation in teacher-led groups on repair of English as a foreign language. Unpublished doctoral dissertation, University of British Columbia.

BREEN, M. 1984, Process in syllabus design. In C. BRUMFIT (ed.) *General English Syllabus Design*. Oxford: Pergamon.
BRINDLEY, G. 1984, *Needs Analysis and Objective-setting in the Adult Migrant Education Program*. Sydney: Adult Migrant Education Service.
BROCK, C. 1986, The effect of referential questions on ESL classroom discourse. *TESOL Quarterly* 20, 47–60.
BROWN, G. and YULE, G. 1983, *Teaching the Spoken Language*. Cambridge: Cambridge University Press.
BRUTON, G. and SAMUDA, V. 1980, Learner and teacher roles in the treatment of oral error in group work. *RELC Journal* 11, 49–63.
BYGATE, M. 1987, *Speaking*. Oxford: Oxford University Press.
CLARKE, M. and SILBERSTEIN, S. 1977, Toward a realization of psycholinguistic principles in the ESL reading class. *Language Learning* 27, 48–65.
DOUGHTY, C. and PICA, T. 1986, 'Information gap' tasks: Do they facilitate second language acquisition? *TESOL Quarterly* 20, 305–25.
DUFF, P. 1986, Another look at interlanguage talk: Taking task to task. In R. Day (ed.) *Talking to Learn: Conversation in Second Language Acquisition*. Rowley, MA: Newbury House.
GREGG, K. 1989, Second language acquisition theory: The case for a generative perspective. In S. GASS and J. SCHACHTER (eds) *Linguistic Perspectives on Second Language Acquisition*. Cambridge: Cambridge University Press.
HALLIDAY, M. A. K. 1985, *An Introduction to Functional Grammar*. London: Edward Arnold.
KUMPF, L. 1984, Temporal systems and universality in language. In F. ECKMAN, L. BELL and D. NELSON (eds) *Universals of Second Language Acquisition*. Rowley, MA: Newbury House.
LARSEN-FREEMAN, D. and LONG, M. H. 1991, *An Introduction to Second Language Acquisition Research*. London: Longman.
LONG, M. H. 1981, Questions in foreigner talk discourse. *Language Learning* 31, 135–57.
—— 1985, A role for instruction in second language acquisition: Task-based language training. In K. HYLTENSTAM and M. PIENEMANN (eds) *Modelling and Assessing Second Language Acquisition*. Clevedon: Multilingual Matters.
LONG, M. H. and CROOKES, G. 1986, Intervention points in second language classroom processes. Paper presented at the RELC Regional Seminar, Singapore, April.
LONG, M. H., ADAMS, L. MCLEAN, M. and CASTAÑOS, F. 1976, Doing things with words: Verbal interaction in lockstep and small groups classroom situations. In R. CRYMES and J. FANSELOW (eds) *On TESOL '76*. Washington DC: TESOL.
MARTIN, J. 1985, *Factual Writing: Exploring and Challenging Social Reality*. Geelong: Deakin University Press.
MONTGOMERY, C. and EISENSTEIN, M. 1982, Real reality revisited: An experimental course in ESL. *TESOL Quarterly* 19(2), 317–34.
MORRIS, A. and STEWART-DORE, N. 1984, *Learning to Learn from Text: Effective Reading in the Content Areas*. Sydney: Addison-Wesley.
NUNAN, D. 1985, Content familiarity and the perception of textual relationships in second language reading. *RELC Journal* 16, 43–51.
—— 1987, Communicative language teaching: Making it work. *ELT Journal* 41, 136–45.
—— 1988a, *Syllabus Design*. Oxford: Oxford University Press.

—— 1988b, *The Learner-Centred Curriculum.* Cambridge: Cambridge University Press.

—— 1988c, Learning strategy preferences by EFL teachers in Southeast Asia. Paper presented at the 4th International Conference, Institute of Language in Education, Hong Kong, 1988.

—— 1989, *Designing Tasks for the Communicative Classroom.* Cambridge: Cambridge University Press.

PORTER, P. 1983, Variations in the conversations of adult learners of English as a function of the proficiency level of the participants. Unpublished PhD dissertation, Stanford University.

PORTER, D and ROBERTS, J. 1981, Authentic listening activities. *ELT Journal* 36, 37–47.

PRABHU, N. 1987, *Second Language Pedagogy.* Oxford: Oxford University Press.

RICHARDS, J., PLATT, J. and WEBER, H. 1985, *Longman Dictionary of Applied Linguistics.* London: Longman.

VARONIS, E. M. and GASS, S. 1985, Nonnative/nonnative conversations: A model for negotiation of meaning. *Applied Linguistics* 6, 71–90.

WIDDOWSON, H. 1987, Aspects of syllabus design. In M. TICKOO (ed.) *Language Syllabuses: State of the Art.* Singapore: RELC.

WILLING, K. 1988, *Learning Styles in Adult Migrant Education.* Adelaide: NCRC.

WRIGHT, T. 1987, *Roles of Teachers and Learners.* Oxford: Oxford University Press.

3 The Name of the Task and the Task of Naming: Methodological Aspects of Task-based Pedagogy

B. KUMARAVADIVELU
San Jose State University

Introduction

Issues concerning task-based pedagogy have recently engaged the minds of several researchers, resulting in a notable surge in the publication of research papers, scholarly books and textbooks dealing with the subject (Breen, 1989; Brown & Palmer, 1988; Candlin & Murphy, 1987; Crookes, 1986; Doughty & Pica, 1986; Duff, 1986; Foley, 1991; Kumaravadivelu, 1991; Long, 1985; Madden & Reinhart, 1987; Nunan, 1989; Prabhu, 1987; Samuda & Madden, 1985; Swales, 1990). In spite of this welcome surge, *task*[1] remains an entity that defies clear terminological, conceptual and methodological understanding largely because of the indiscriminate, non-descript use of the term. A close reading of the current literature on task-based pedagogy makes it difficult to determine a set of governing principles or even defining criteria commonly shared by all.[2]

One of the references cited above, Crookes (1986), is a laudable, and to my knowledge the only, attempt at a comprehensive cross-disciplinary review of *task* and task classification. The review rightly points out that *task* has been vaguely and variously defined and that there are problems in the way it has been used. But the review does not consider in detail the terminological, conceptual and methodological ambiguity that the vague and various uses of the term seem to have created in the areas of classroom procedures, syllabus design and materials production. What I propose to do in this chapter, therefore, is to attempt to (a) highlight the terminological and

69

conceptual ambiguity concerning the use of *task*, (b) argue that *task* relates more to methodological procedures than to syllabus design, (c) redefine *task* with specific reference to major categories of language teaching approaches, and (d) discuss ways in which the practicing teacher can be helped to make informed choices about task analysis and task selection. Thus the primary intention (or, should I say, task?) of this chapter is to address several terminological, conceptual and methodological issues related to the notion of task and task-based pedagogy, and to make suggestions for critical consideration and further exploration.

Terminological and Conceptual Ambiguity

In the current literature on second/foreign language (L2), teaching, a series of context-free and context-sensitive definitions occur over the term *task*. These definitions range from simple generality to complex specificity, from everyday tasks performed in the 'real-world'[3] to pedagogical tasks performed in the L2 classroom. The most general of all is probably the one proposed by Long (1985) in the context of 'real-world' tasks. He defines task as

> A piece of work undertaken for oneself or for others, freely or for some reward. Thus, examples of task include painting a fence, dressing a child, filling out a form . . . in other words, by 'task' is meant the hundred and one things people *do* in everyday life, at work, at play, and in between. (Long, 1985: 89; emphasis as in the original)

Moving away from the outside society and into the educational community, Crookes (1986) and Wright (1987) define task from the perspective of general education. For Crookes, task is

> a piece of work or an activity, usually with a specified objective, undertaken as part of an educational course, at work, or used to elicit data for research. (Crookes, 1986: 1)

Wright takes a similar view. His tasks are 'instructional questions which ask, demand or even invite learners (or teachers) to perform operations on input data' (Wright, 1987: 48). Moving still closer to the narrow world of the L2 learner, Krahnke (1987: 57) looks at tasks as things that are performed by L2 learners in class as a rehearsal for social communication outside the classroom. He says

> the defining characteristic of task-based content is that it uses activities that the learners have to do for non-instructional purposes outside of

the classroom as opportunities for language learning. Tasks are distinct from other activities to the degree that they have non-instructional purposes. (Krahnke, 1987: 67)

Definitions geared more specifically towards the instructional role of tasks with particular reference to language development in the formalized and ritualized world of the L2 classroom have been attempted, among others, by Breen (1987), Candlin (1987), Nunan (1989) and Swales (1990). Breen defines task as

A range of workplans which have the overall purpose of facilitating language learning — from the simple and brief exercise type to more complex and lengthy activities such as group problem-solving or simulations and decision-making. (Breen, 1987: 23)

Candlin offers by far the most complex and comprehensive definition, and in doing so, he has elegantly built into the definition several variables that appear to play a crucial role in constituting an instructional task. Task, according to him, is

one of a set of differentiated, sequencable, problem-posing activities involving learners' cognitive and communicative procedures applied to existing and new knowledge in the collective exploration and pursuance of foreseen or emergent goals within a social milieu. (Candlin 1987: 10)

Following Candlin's insights[4] and introducing yet another important variable, genre, Swales defines *task* as

one of a set of differentiated, sequencable goal-directed activities drawing upon a range of cognitive and communicative procedures relatable to the acquisition of pre-genre and genre skills appropriate to a foreseen or emerging sociorhetorical situation. (Swales, 1990: 76)

Without explicitly getting into several variables embodied in the definitions given by Candlin and Swales but remaining within the realm of the L2 classroom, Nunan (1989: 10, Chapter 2 this volume) proposes a particular type of tasks called 'communicative tasks' — tasks that involve communicative language use. He defines a communicative task as

a piece of classroom work which involves learners in comprehending, manipulating, producing or interacting in the target language while their attention is principally focused on meaning rather than form. (Nunan, 1989: 10)

It is evident that the multiplicity of definitions and interpretations related to *task* and task-based pedagogy is the result of several scholars working from a number of different perspectives, all undoubtedly contributing to the emerging concept of *task* and task-based pedagogy. This multiplicity of approaches to *task* carries at once the prospect of enriching our understanding of *task* and task-based pedagogy, and also the potential to cloud, if not confuse, task-related issues that need to be investigated in greater detail.

It appears to me that a major part of the conceptual and terminological ambiguity arises because of at least two distinctly recognizable trends one can discern in the current literature. The first trend relates to the dichotomy between content and methodology of language teaching. That is, the term *task* is often used with reference to both linguistic *content* and classroom *methodology* of L2 teaching, thereby conflating the distinction between the two. The second trend relates to the distinction between language teaching approaches. That is, the term is used in relation to various language teaching approaches regardless of the diverse governing principles and classroom procedures that distinguish one approach from another. I shall discuss below these two trends in detail.

Task in Relation to Methodology and Content

A traditional and still popular belief holds that methodology refers to the *how* of language teaching and content refers to the *what* of language teaching. The latter has come to be known as syllabus. A syllabus is widely recognized as a preplanned, preordained, presequenced inventory of linguistic specifications imposed in most cases on teachers and learners whereas methodology is a course of action practicing teachers follow or are advised/expected to follow in the realization of syllabus specifications. In other words, 'syllabus as a source of teacher reference can only effect learning through methodological mediation' (Widdowson, 1990: 130). In practice, syllabus specifications and classroom methodology need not, and they usually do not, adhere to one and the same psycho-sociolinguistic and educational principles governing L2 development. Hence, as Widdowson (1984, 1987, 1990) has persistently argued, it is perfectly possible to adopt a communicative methodology in the realization of a structural syllabus.[5]

The dichotomy between content and methodology is better understood historically. As Stern (1987) points out, during the 1950s, a movement began that focused less on classroom methodology and more on teaching objectives, linguistic content and curricular design. Stern (1987: 20) sees this movement as 'a reaction against the persistent preoccupation in language pedagogy with teaching method' that existed during the preceding era. With the advent of the audiolingual approach, language pedagogy became predominantly content-driven. Now, with the emerging task-based pedagogy, the pendulum appears to be swinging back to methodology. This historical development can be characterized in the form of a continuum as shown in Figure 1.

Content $<$ _ Form based _ Function based _ Task based _$>$ Method
driven   pedagogy   pedagogy   pedagogy   driven

FIGURE 1   *Content/method continuum*

In a predominantly content-driven pedagogy, such as a structural approach, teachers and learners were presented with a preselected, presequenced syllabus, the realization of which constituted the primary, perhaps the only, objective of classroom activity. Teachers ostensibly knew what they were supposed to teach and learners ostensibly knew what they were supposed to learn — mainly because structural textbooks carried, at the beginning of every lesson, a list of grammar and vocabulary items which were the focus of that particular lesson. Thus, content becomes the central tenet of a structural approach.

In a predominantly method-driven pedagogy, such as task-based pedagogy, teachers and learners have a remarkable degree of flexibility, for they are presented with a set of general learning objectives and problem-solving tasks, and not a list of specific linguistic items. The essence of a task-based methodology lies in the negotiated interactional opportunity given to learners to navigate their own paths and routes to learning, using their own learning styles and learning strategies. Learning outcome then is the result of a fairly unpredictable interaction between the learner, the task and the task situation (Breen, 1987). Furthermore, as Foley (1991) argues from the Vygotskyan psycholinguistic perspective, task-based L2 learning is an internal, self-regulating process which will vary according to the individual and cannot specifically be controlled by the syllabus designer or the classroom teacher. It is, however, the teacher's responsibility to promote and maximize learning opportunities through adequate and appropriate classroom methodological procedures. Thus, methodology becomes the central tenet of task-based pedagogy.

An alternative view of the content/methodology dichotomy in the context of task-based pedagogy is given by Nunan (1989) who argues:

If we maintain the traditional distinction between syllabus design and methodology, seeing syllabus design as being primarily concerned with the specification of what learners will learn, and methodology as being mainly concerned with specifying how learners will learn, then the design of learning tasks is part of methodology. However, if we see curriculum planning as an integrated set of processes involving, among other things, the specification of both what and how, then the argument over whether the design and development of tasks belongs to syllabus design or to methodology becomes unimportant. (Nunan, 1989: 1)

While I agree with Nunan that a task-based curriculum should reflect an integrated set of processes, I nevertheless see task-based pedagogy to be predominantly method-driven as I have attempted to explain in this section. In fact, if I understand it correctly, Nunan's own definition of the communicative task is, in my terminology, method-driven even though he believes that the dichotomy between syllabus and methodology is unimportant. Recall Nunan's definition (1989: 10) cited earlier and repeated here: a communicative task is 'a piece of classroom work which involves learners in comprehending, manipulating, producing or interacting in the target language while their attention is principally focused on meaning rather than form'. As the key words in the definition testify, his task-based pedagogy puts a lot of premium on classroom methodological teacher/learner activities such as comprehension, manipulation, production, interaction and attention to meaning rather than form — all characteristics of a method-driven pedagogy. That is, the communicative task as defined by him makes sense in the specific context of a meaning-focused, interactional methodology rather than a form-focused methodology.

Since *task* is so closely intertwined with classroom methodology, it seems to me that one way of dealing with the conceptual and terminological ambiguity discussed earlier is to redefine it in relation to specific language teaching methodologies so that it reflects the fundamental concepts governing language teaching methodologies generally in use. Such a redefinition will probably contribute to clear the terminological and conceptual ambiguity surrounding language learning tasks and to make our investigation and discussion of task-based pedagogy more meaningful and productive. Before I attempt to redefine *task* in relation to language teaching methodologies, it is worth making a detour to offer a brief review of the fundamental concepts of current language teaching approaches.

Language Teaching Approaches

For the immediate purpose of determining the nature and purpose of language learning tasks, it appears useful to classify language teaching approaches into three broad categories:[6] (a) language-centered approaches, (b) learner-centered approaches and (c) learning-centered approaches. As the terms suggest, language-centered approaches are those which are principally concerned with linguistic forms. These approaches (such as the audiolingual approach) seeks to provide opportunities for learners to practice preselected, presequenced linguistic structures through form-focused activities in class, assuming that the learners can draw from this linguistic repertoire whenever they wish to communicate in the target languages outside the class.

Learner-centered approaches are those which are principally concerned with learner needs. These approaches (such as communicative approaches) seek to provide opportunities for learners to practice preselected, presequenced notions and functions through communication-focused activities, assuming that the learners can make use of them to fulfil their communicative needs outside the class.

Learning-centered approaches are those which are principally concerned with the psycholinguistic processes of L2 learning/teaching. These approaches (such as the natural approach — Krashen & Terrell, 1983) provide opportunities for learners to participate in open-ended interaction through meaning-focused activities in class, assuming that the learners can develop grammatical ability through those meaning-focused activities.

It is essential to remind ourselves of the important ways in which these three approaches are similar to, and different from, each other. The two basic principles that typically characterize a language-centered approach are: first, it treats L2 learning as a linear, additive process. In other words, it was believed that an L2 develops primarily in terms of what Rutherford (1987) calls 'accumulated entities' and that the teacher's responsibility is to introduce, one at a time, an inventory of linguistic items. Second, language-centered methodologists advocated explicit introduction, analysis and explanation of linguistic systems. They did not seem to be concerned with the type of questions eloquently recaptured by Rutherford:

> the most brilliant linguists can as yet come nowhere near knowing fully what constitute the proper generalizations and the correct formulations for the rules of English syntax, then, how can anything of this sort, in whatever 'simplified' form, be profitably 'taught' by any teacher or 'learned' by any learner? (Rutherford, 1987: 17)

In other words, they did not seem to be concerned about the fact that these systems are too complex and our explanatory principles too inadequate to be of any significant help for form-focused learning/teaching operations (for a detailed critique, see Chomsky, 1976, 1980; Prabhu, 1987; Rutherford, 1987).

The perceived failure of language-centered approaches to help L2 learners become both grammatically accurate and communicatively fluent gradually led us to learner-centered approaches. Learner-oriented methodologists kept in mind the L2 learner's language use in social interaction or for academic study, and presented linguistic structures in communicative contexts. However, at the theoretical core of learner-centered approaches are the same two basic principles that characterized language-centered approaches. In spite of a strong theoretical foundation which emphasized the cyclical and analytical nature of communicative syllabuses (as, for instance, discussed in Wilkins, 1976; Munby, 1978), learner-centered approaches remain, basically, linear and additive. Besides, proponents of learner-centered approaches, like those of language-centered approaches, believe in accumulated entities. The one major difference is that in the case of language-centered methodology, the accumulated entities stand for linguistic structures, and in the case of learner-centered methodology, they stand for structures plus notions/functions. Just as language-centered methodologists believed that the linguistic structures of a language could be sequentially presented and explained, the learner-centered methodologists also believed that each notional/functional category could be matched with one or more linguistic forms which could be sequentially presented and explained to L2 learners. (Again, for a detailed critique see Paulston, 1985; Prabhu 1987; Rutherford, 1987.)

The basic principles governing learning-centered approaches, however, are fundamentally different from the two basic principles governing both language- and learner-centered approaches. According to learning-centered methodologists, L2 development is a nonlinear process and, therefore, does not need preselected, presequenced systematic language inputs but requires the creation of conditions in which learners engage in meaningful interaction in class. They also believe that language is best learned/taught when the learners' attention is focused on understanding, saying and doing something with language, and not when their attention is focused explicitly on linguistic features. In other words, for language- and learner-centered methodologists, L2 development is primarily *intentional* or direct but for learning-centered methodologists, L2 development is primarily *incidental* or indirect.[7]

In seeking to redress what they considered to be the two fundamental flaws that characterized previous approaches, learning-centered methodologists also seek to fill what Long (1985: 79) calls 'a psycholinguistic vacuum'. That is, they claim to derive insights from psycholinguistic research on L2 development and attempt to incorporate those insights into second language pedagogy. As a result, the changes they advocate relate not just to syllabus specifications — as it happened in the case of our shift from language-centered to learner-centered pedagogy — but to all aspects of learning/teaching operations: syllabus design, materials production, classroom methodology, formative/summative evaluation and teacher education.

Task in Relation to Language Teaching Approaches

Having briefly described the fundamental characteristics of major language teaching approaches, I shall now turn to the connection between the concept of *task* and language teaching approaches. As I pointed out earlier, the ambiguity surrounding *task* is not just terminological; it is conceptual too. That is, not every researcher conceives the nature, scope and purpose of task-based pedagogy in the same way. Samuda & Madden (1985), for instance, remark that their task design incorporates a built-in language focus in which aspects of the linguistic code can be explicitly dealt with. Similarly, Krahnke (1987: 58–9), while observing that explicit metalinguistic knowledge may not be addressed by task-based instruction, nevertheless advocates that if such knowledge is a desired outcome of instruction, then task-based learning can be combined with more traditional types of instructional activities associated with language-centered approaches.

Task-based pedagogies proposed by Candlin & Murphy reflect the theoretical principles of learner-centered approaches. For them,

task-based learning continues with and develops recent attention to learner-centered approaches, and in particular the ideas of differentiation and learner interdependence. (Candlin & Murphy, 1987: 3)

The central process they are concerned with is language learning, and

tasks present this in the form of a problem-solving negotiation between knowledge that the learner holds and new knowledge. This activity is conducted through language in use, which may itself be seen as a negotiation of meaning. (Candlin & Murphy: 1987: 1)

The proposals of Krashen (1982), Krashen & Terrell (1983) and Prabhu (1985a, 1987) are consistent with the theoretical principles of learning-centered approaches. They believe, as mentioned earlier, that language is best taught when it is being used to transmit messages, not when it is explicitly taught for conscious learning. Accordingly their tasks are meaning-focused activities in which learners are preoccupied with the process of understanding, extending or conveying meaning, and cope with language forms only incidentally and as demanded by that process.

This description of tasks versus language teaching approaches might lead (rather mislead) readers to conclude that the treatment of tasks and task-based pedagogy in the literature falls neatly into the three categories of language teaching approaches. That certainly is not the case. Samuda & Madden, for instance, say that their task-based learning (TBL)

> is based on the belief that language can be learned by doing, when attention is focused on meaning. TBL therefore, organizes the learning process by tasks to be performed in the target language, not by functions, notions, topics and structures. (Samuda & Madden, 1985: 84)

This is clearly a principle which is in tune with the philosophy of learning-centered methodology. However, some of the task-based instructional materials designed by Samuda & Madden (1985) and Madden & Reinhart (1987) are based on insights drawn from language-centered methodology in that they focus explicitly on certain linguistic items. Interestingly, if we look at the content pages of two ESL textbooks, one following language-centered methodology (Yorkey *et al.*, 1985 [see Appendix 1]), and the other following task-based methodology (Madden & Reinhart, 1987) [Appendix 2]), we find linguistic items and communicative activities listed in both, though not in the same order. To be fair to Madden & Reinhart, it must be pointed out that, as extracts of lesson units from both books amply illustrate, classroom activities designed for the language-centered textbook (Appendix 1a) focus mostly and directly on linguistic features whereas classroom activities designed for the task-based textbook (Appendix 2a) focus mostly on communicative function, and linguistic features are introduced only indirectly.

Samuda & Madden justify this combination of explicit grammar-focused activity and meaning-focused task by saying that

> in order to be responsive to the needs of the students in their program, we have attempted to strike a balance between the dual roles students take on in the classroom: that of language user and that of language learner. (Samuda & Madden, 1985: 84)

The dual approach followed here in order to make a distinction between language *user* and language *learner* appears to be redundant in the context of learning-centered task-based pedagogy according to which L2 learners are supposed to learn their target language by using it meaningfully through negotiated interaction. In other words, the defining phrase is 'learn the language by using it' and not 'learn now, use later'.

Candlin (1987: 10) also seems to take a view which combines instructional task design principles of more than one specific language teaching approach. While discussing the criteria for 'good' language learning tasks, he says that the tasks 'should provide opportunities for language practice' — a characteristic of language-centered methodology. He also points out that 'it would be ironic if a task-based syllabus merely made learners expert at following preset paths and did not promote their own capacities to draw their own maps' (p. 17) — a principle one would associate with learning-centered approaches. Breen also argues that

> a language learning task is also about communication and its codes and conventions; its content can offer data on language and information about language. The content of language tasks can, therefore, be metacommunicative because its subject-matter is directly or indirectly about the means of communication and about the workings of language in use. A grammar exercise, a graded reading, or a written dialogue will serve to exemplify the workings of language by using messages to carry and reveal the code. Alternately, a problem-solving task based upon a sample of target language in use may exploit the code as a means to involve the learner in interpreting and expressing meanings. (Breen, 1987: 28)

What we see here is a focus on grammar exercises, communicative activities and negotiation and expression of meaning — in short, an amalgamation of principles and procedures from all the three language teaching approaches.

Three Categories of Classroom Methodological Procedures

Such then is the richness of interpretation that we come across in the current literature on *task* and task-based pedagogy. In order to put these interpretations into a broad and coherent perspective and also to clarify the terminological and conceptual ambiguity, I suggest a two-step strategy. The first step involves distinguishing three categories of classroom methodological procedures[8] and the second involves hierarchizing them.

In accordance with the fundamental concepts of the three language teaching approaches discussed earlier, classroom methodological procedures can be grouped under three broad categories: (1) language-centered procedures, (2) learner-centered procedures, and (3) learning-centered procedures. In what follows, I attempt to define each of these categories.

In the context of L2 learning and teaching, language centered procedures are operationally defined as a series of *structural exercises* which draw the learners' attention explicitly to the formal properties of language, and the learners are required to do these exercises by using specific grammatical or vocabulary items that are introduced to them through preselection and pre-sequencing, with the view to leading them along a predetermined path and towards a predetermined goal. Sample instructional materials provided in Appendix 1 illustrate this category of methodological procedures.

Learner-centered procedures are operationally defined as a series of *communicative activities* in which the learners' attention is explicitly focused on formal as well as functional properties of language and they are required to engage in these activities by using specific formal, functional and notional properties that are introduced to them through preselection and pre-sequencing, with the view to leading them along a predetermined path and towards a predetermined goal. Sample instructional materials provided in Appendix 2 illustrate this category.

Learning-centered procedures are operationally defined as a series of *pedagogic tasks* in which learners' attention is focused on negotiation of meaning and they are required to perform the tasks by self-deploying any or all linguistic repertoire they have developed at that point in time, with the view to leading them along an open-ended path, but towards a predetermined goal. Sample instructional materials provided in Appendix 3 illustrate this category.

These three categories of classroom procedures can be related in terms of a hierarchy, as shown in Figure 2.

Pedagogic tasks —> Communicative activities —> Structural exercises

FIGURE 2   *A hierarchy of classroom procedures*

This hierarchy of classroom procedures is interpreted to mean that learning-centered, *pedagogic tasks* include some of the characteristics of learner-centered *communicative activities* which in turn include some of the characteristics of language-centered *structural exercises*. In other words, from a learning/teaching point of view, *tasks* have a broader and more comprehensive scope than *activities* which in turn have a broader and more comprehensive scope than *exercises*.

A learning-centered task-based pedagogy enjoys comprehensiveness because its theoretical principles and classroom procedures, unlike those of language- and learner-centered pedagogies, are basically grounded in currently available insights derived from psycholinguistic research on L2 development. As such, the designing of tasks has to take into consideration, minimally, the following psycholinguistic principles:[9] language learning is a developmental process; it is a decision-making process; it is a process of negotiation; it is not linear and additive; it is primarily incidental; it is largely a subconscious activity, and it is a meaning-focused activity. It is not the purpose of this chapter to go into the merits of these psycholinguistic insights; interested readers can find useful argumentation compiled and presented in, among others, Candlin & Murphy (1987), Ellis (1990), Hutchinson & Waters (1987), Krashen (1982), Prabhu (1987), Tarone & Yule (1989), Widdowson (1990), and the references cited therein. Instead, I shall briefly highlight certain issues of learning-centered, task-based pedagogy, which arise out of its psycholinguistic orientation. Specifically, I shall deal with issues concerning task-based classroom procedures.

Task-based Classroom Procedures

The psycholinguistic principles of learning-centered task-based pedagogy briefly described above pose a considerable challenge to the ingenuity of the practicing teacher who will have significantly reduced help from the twin 'crutches' that came neatly packaged with earlier pedagogies: prescribed textbooks and presequenced syllabus specifications. Designing language learning tasks entails a vast amount of imagination and creativity on the part of syllabus and materials designers. There cannot be a set of syllabus specifications as we know them in traditional language teaching experience. Likewise, instructional materials can be only an indication of content in the form of tasks, problems and scenarios leaving the actual language to be negotiated in each classroom. In other words, we ought to think in terms of *learning* materials rather than *teaching* materials, as suggested by Allwright (1981). Second, as Prabhu (1987: 94) points out, any collection of instructional materials can have only the status of *source books* rather than *course books*. How would such a source book look? Appendix 4 provides sample materials from a book by Brown & Palmer (1988) that represents an attempt at producing a task-based source book. One section gives a list of ideas; another provides what the authors call 'developed activities'. These are very general suggestions for classroom teachers about what can actually be done in class. The book provides only content and no language items. The language that is needed to perform the task has to be negotiated by the learner in the process of carrying out these tasks with, of course, help from the teacher whose job it is to facilitate learning opportunities in class.

The teacher's job as facilitator of learning opportunities through learner interaction and expression is complicated by the fact that tasks most often do not, on the surface, represent any scale of cognitive, communicative or linguistic complexity. It is up to the teacher to choose a set of tasks, adopt or adapt them to suit the specific learner needs, wants and situations, and present them in a sequence that makes pedagogic sense. This is easier said than done because sequencing of linguistic input, whether grammatical, notional/functional or task-based, has always been done based on intuitive considerations rather than on any principled and proven way (Crookes, 1986; Long, 1985; Stern, 1987). From a practical pedagogic point of view, our rationale for sequencing input is no more informed and objective today than it was a quarter century ago when Mackey (1965) discussed the highly subjective notions of 'difficulty' and 'complexity' in the context of selection and gradation.[10]

Such a lack of informed and objective criteria for sequencing linguistic input, however, need not be a hinderance to task-based instruction. Sequencing becomes a crucial component of L2 learning/teaching operations only in language-centered and learner-centered approaches which are predominantly content-driven. In a predominantly method-driven approach such as task-based pedagogy, the question of sequencing becomes peripheral since what is of paramount importance is classroom methodology rather than linguistic content. Consequently, the right place where decision concerning sequencing should be made is the classroom and the right person to make those decisions is the practicing teacher. This does not mean that the practicing teacher is left with no prior guidance whatsoever. Task-based methodologists seek to give the practicing teacher what Lee (1987: 42), in a related context, calls a 'pre-syllabus' consisting of an inventory of tasks, problems and scenarios, and an indication of the options available at each point where decisions have to be made. They also seek to provide the teacher with the knowledge and skills necessary to make informed choices about *task* and task sequencing.

Making Informed Choices through Task Analysis

One of the ways in which the practicing teacher can be helped to make informed choices about tasks and task sequences is through task analysis. Task-based methodologists have made some useful suggestions for analyzing task. These suggestions, as I understand them, can be classified under four broad rationales: a communicative rationale (Krahnke, 1987), a pedagogic rationale (Long, 1985; Prabhu, 1987; Widdowson, 1987, 1990), a psycho-social rationale (Breen, 1987, 1989; Candlin, 1987) and an integrative rationale (Bygate, 1987; Nunan, 1989, Chapter 2 this volume). The communicative rationale (dubbed the 'real-world' rationale in the literature) is concerned with language learning tasks that treat classroom activity as a rehearsal for actual communicative behavior in the outside world. These tasks are usually based on needs analyses of communicative performance in non-academic settings. The pedagogic rationale is concerned with language learning tasks that form the basis of classroom activities for teachers and students. These tasks may be unrelated to communicative performance in the outside world. The psycho-social rationale is concerned with language learning tasks that take into consideration cognitive, expressive and social parameters. These tasks are generally the outcome of a negotiated interaction between the participants involved in the activities of the L2 classroom which is considered a mini-society with its own rules, rights and responsibilities. The integrated rationale is concerned with language learning tasks that, in a principled way, bring together major characteristics of the other three rationale.

Yet another rationale which, in my view, needs to be taken into account along with the others is what I call the classroom interactional rationale. It is concerned with aspects of teacher intention and learner interpretation of language learning tasks. The match and the mismatch between teacher intention and learner interpretation of language learning tasks become crucial because of the importance given to interaction and negotiation in the task-based classroom (see Samuda & Rounds, this volume, and Shortreed, companion volume). Learning-centered task-based pedagogy minimizes the role of the syllabus designer (in the sense that the syllabus designer can provide only a 'pre-syllabus') and the materials producer (in the sense that the materials producer can provide only a 'source book') and conversely, maximizes the role of the teacher and the learner. The teacher and the learner have a remarkable degree of flexibility as well as responsibility, for they are presented only with a set of general learning objectives and language learning tasks to be jointly interpreted in the classroom as the classroom interactional process evolves. This lays a heavy emphasis on learner/teacher perceptions of classroom aims and events thereby increasing the potential for misunderstanding and miscommunication.

It is therefore important that the practicing teacher is sensitized to the potential mismatch between teacher intention and learner interpretation. In order to help the teacher learn to analyze tasks from this particular class-

84   TASKS IN A PEDAGOGICAL CONTEXT

room interactional perspective, I have elsewhere (Kumaravadivelu, 1991) identified ten potential sources of mismatch which can form the basis for task analysis. These sources are:

1. *Cognitive:* A source which refers to the knowledge of the world and mental processes through which learners obtain conceptual understanding of physical and natural phenomena.

2. *Communicative:* A source which refers to skills through which learners exchange messages, including the use of communication strategies.

3. *Linguistic:* A source which refers to linguistic repertoire — syntactic, semantic and pragmatic knowledge of the target language — that is minimally required to problem-solve.

4. *Pedagogic:* A source which refers to teacher/learner perceptions about stated or unstated, short- and/or long-term objective(s) of language learning tasks.

5. *Strategic:* A source which refers to learning strategies, that is, operations, steps, plans and routines used by the learner to facilitate the obtaining, storage, retrieval and use of information.

6. *Cultural:* A source which refers to prior knowledge of the target culture norms minimally required for the learner to understand the language learning tasks and solve the problem.

7. *Evaluative:* A source which refers to articulated or unarticulated types and modes of ongoing self-evaluation measures used by learners to monitor their progress in their language learning.

8. *Procedural:* A source which refers to stated or unstated paths chosen by the learner to problem-solve. A procedural source pertains to locally-specified, currently identified, bottom-up tactics which seek an immediate resolution to a specific problem on hand; whereas, strategic source, mentioned earlier, pertains to a broad-based, higher-level, top-down strategy which seeks an overall solution to a general language learning situation.

9. *Instructional:* A source which refers to instructional directions given by the teacher and/or indicated by the textbook writer to help learners problem-solve.

10. *Attitudinal:* A source which refers to participants' attitudes towards the nature and second/foreign language learning and teaching, the nature of classroom culture, and teacher/learner role expectations.

In my view, the five rationales for task analysis are not contradictory; in fact, they are complementary to each other making up for whatever limitations each might have. The potential of each rationale or a combination thereof for task analysis, task selection and task sequence is yet to be fully explored. They certainly carry the promise of helping the practicing teacher understand the nature, the scope and the interpretive density of language learning tasks. What is needed is a set of strategies that can be incorporated into preservice and inservice teacher education programs in order to equip teachers with the knowledge and skills necessary to do task analysis. Much remains to be done.

Conclusion

In this chapter, I have attempted to highlight the terminological and conceptual ambiguity concerning the use of *task* and argued that *task* is more a methodological construct than a curricular one. I have tried to redefine *task* with specific reference to major categories of language teaching approaches and to explore the task-based classroom procedures with the view to helping the practicing teacher make informed choices about task analysis and task selection. I have also attempted to raise doubts and questions regarding several research problems that need to be explored further in order to reach the level of knowledge and confidence that is required to implement a learning-centered task-based pedagogy.

Notes

1. *Task* in italics refers to the concept of task while task without italics refers to language learning tasks of different types.
2. Sometimes the term is used merely because it is in vogue. At least one researcher, Coleman (1987: 145), quite candidly remarks: 'originally, we used the name "activity" rather than "task". Being rather out of touch with what was happening elsewhere, we were unaware that "task" was becoming a vogue term.' So saying he goes on to use the term task wherever he would perhaps have used 'exercise' or 'activity'.
3. The phrase 'real-world' widely used in the literature to refer to the world outside the classroom, suggests that the L2 classroom does not represent a real world, a suggestion I disagree with. Therefore, I put 'real-world' in quotes.
4. See Swales (1990: 74–6) for a detailed critique of Candlin's idea of a task.
5. See Stern (1987) and Yalden (1987) for a different perspective.

6. This classification of language teaching approaches is not entirely new. See Prabhu, 1985b and Hutchinson & Waters, 1987. Prabhu suggested the term 'Learning-centered approach' in the context of the Bangalore Communicational Teaching Project (see also Prabhu, 1987). Hutchinson & Waters suggested the three categories of language teaching approaches in the context of English for specific purposes. I do not see any reason why the same classification cannot be applied to general purpose second language pedagogy as well.
7. See Snow (1987) for a more detailed discussion on intentional/incidental learning.
8. By *procedures*, I mean a set of teaching strategies indicated by the syllabus designer and the materials producer and adopted/adapted by the practicing teacher in order to realize the language learning and teaching objectives. I use this term in contrast to *principles*, by which I mean a set of insights derived from theories of linguistic sciences, psychology and other allied feeder disciplines that govern various aspects of language development and language teaching approaches.
9. Adapted from Hutchinson & Waters (1987).
10. Empirical research such as morpheme studies (Dulay & Burt, 1974; Krashen, Madden & Bailey, 1975), implicational universals studies (Gass, 1979; Pavesi, 1984; Zobl, 1983), learnability/teachability hypothesis studies (Pienemann, 1985, 1987) are yet to provide us with a set of psycholinguistically valid criteria that can be applied for sequencing linguistic input for an entire L2 learning and teaching program. See also Ellis (1990) and Widdowson (1990) for detailed critiques of such studies.

References

ALLWRIGHT, R. L. 1981, What do we want teaching materials for? *ELT Journal* 36, 5–18.
BREEN, M. P. 1987, Learner contributions to task design. In C. N. CANDLIN and D. F. MURPHY (eds) *Language Learning Tasks* (pp. 23–46). London: Prentice-Hall International.
—— 1989, The evaluation cycle for language learning tasks. In R. K. JOHNSON (ed.) *The Second Language Curriculum* (pp. 187–206). Cambridge: Cambridge University Press.
BROWN, J. M. and PALMER, A. S. 1988, *The Listening Approach: Methods and Materials for Applying Krashen's Input Hypothesis.* London: Longman.
BYGATE, M. 1987, *Speaking.* Oxford: Oxford University Press.
CANDLIN, C. N. 1987, Towards task-based language learning. In C. N. CANDLIN and D. F. MURPHY (eds) *Language Learning Tasks* (pp. 5–22). London: Prentice-Hall International.
CANDLIN, C. N. and MURPHY, D. F. (eds) 1987, *Language Learning Tasks.* Prentice-Hall International.
CHOMSKY, N. 1976, *Reflections on Language.* London: Temple Smith.
—— 1980, *Rules and Representations.* Oxford: Basil Blackwell.

COLEMAN, H. 1987, 'Little tasks make large return': Task-based language learning in large crowds. In C. N. CANDLIN and D. F. MURPHY (eds) *Language Learning Tasks* (pp. 121–46). London: Prentice-Hall International.

CROOKES, G. 1986, Task classification: A cross-disciplinary review. Center for Second Language Classroom Research, Social Science Research Institute, University of Hawai'i.

DOUGHTY, C. and PICA, T. 1986, Information gap tasks: Do they facilitate second language acquisition? *TESOL Quarterly* 20, 305–25.

DUFF, P. 1986, Another look at interlanguage talk: Taking task to task. In R. DAY (ed.) *Talking to Learn* (pp. 147–81). Rowley MA: Newbury House.

DULAY, H. and BURT, M. 1974, Natural sequences in child second language acquisition. *Language Learning* 24, 37–53.

ELLIS, R. 1990, *Instructed Second Language Acquisition*. Cambridge: Basil Blackwell.

FOLEY, J. 1991, A psycholinguistic framework for task-based approaches to language teaching. *Applied Linguistics* 12, 62–75.

GASS, S. 1979, Language transfer and universal grammatical relations. *Language Learning* 27, 327–44.

HUTCHINSON, T. and WATERS, A. 1987, *English for Specific Purposes: A Learning-centered Approach*. Cambridge: Cambridge University Press.

KRAHNKE, K. 1987, *Approaches to Syllabus Design for Foreign Language Teaching*. Englewood, NJ: Prentice-Hall, Inc.

KRASHEN, S. 1982, *Principles and Practice in Second Language Acquisition*. Oxford: Pergamon Press.

KRASHEN, S. and TERRELL, T. 1983, *The Natural Approach*. San Francisco, CA: The Alemany Press.

KRASHEN, S., MADDEN, C. and BAILEY, K. 1975, Theoretical aspects of grammatical sequencing. In M. BURT and H. DULAY (eds) *Second Language Learning, Teaching and Bilingual Education* (pp. 44–55). Washington, DC: TESOL.

KUMARAVADIVELU, B. 1991, Language learning tasks: Teacher intention and learner interpretation. *ELT Journal* 45, 98–17.

LEE, W. R. 1987, Some thoughts on the make-up of language teaching syllabuses. In M. L. TICKOO (ed.) *Language Syllabuses: State of the Art* (pp. 39–43). Singapore: Regional Language Centre.

LONG, M. H. 1985, A role for instruction in second language acquisition: Task-based language training. In K. HYLTENSTAM and M. PIENEMANN (eds) *Modelling and Assessing Second Language Acquisition* (pp. 77–100). Clevedon: Multilingual Matters.

MACKEY, W. F. 1965, *Language Teaching Analysis*. Bloomington: Indiana University Press.

MADDEN, C. and REINHART, S. M. 1987, *Pyramids. Structurally Based Tasks for ESL Learners*. Ann Arbor: The University of Michigan Press.

MUNBY, J. 1978, *Communicative Syllabus Design*. Cambridge: Cambridge University Press.

NUNAN, D. 1989, *Designing Tasks for the Communicative Classroom*. Cambridge: Cambridge University Press.

PAULSTON, C. B. 1985, Communicative competence and language teaching: Second thoughts. In B K. DAS (ed.) *Communicative Language Teaching* (pp. 14–31). Singapore: Singapore University Press.

PAVESI, M. 1984, The acquisition of relative clauses in a formal and in an informal setting: Further evidence in support of the markedness hypothesis. In D. SINGLETON, and D. LITTLE (eds) *Language Learning in Formal and Informal Contexts*. Dublin: IRAAL.

PIENEMANN, M. 1985, Learnability and syllabus construction. In K. HYLTENSTAM and M. PIENEMANN (eds) *Modelling and Assessing Second Language Acquisition* (pp. 23–76). Clevedon: Multilingual Matters.

—— 1987, Psychological constraints on the teachability of languages. In C. PFAFF (ed.) *First and Second Language Acquisition Processes* (pp. 143–68). Rowley, MA: Newbury House.

PRABHU, N. S. 1985a, Communicative teaching: Communicative in what sense? In B. K. DAS (ed.) *Communicative Language Teaching* (pp. 32–40). Singapore: Singapore University Press.

—— 1985b, Coping with the unknown in language pedagogy. In R. QUIRK and H. G. WIDDOWSON (eds) *English in the World: Teaching and Learning the Language and Literatures* (pp. 164–73). Cambridge: Cambridge University Press.

—— 1987, *Second Language Pedagogy*. Oxford: Oxford University Press.

RUTHERFORD, W. 1987, *Second Language Grammar: Learning and Teaching*. London: Longman.

SAMUDA, V. and MADDEN, C. 1985, Task-based test: Testing as a reflection of classroom methodology. *Papers in Applied Linguistics — Michigan*. 1, 84–94.

SNOW, C. 1987, Beyond conversation: Second language learners' acquisition of description and explanation. In J. P. LANTOFF and A. LABARCA (eds) *Research in Second Language Learning* (pp. 3–16). New Jersey: Ablex.

STERN, H. H. 1987. Directions in syllabus design. In M. L. TICKOO (ed.) *Language Syllabuses: State of the Art* (pp. 19–32). Singapore: Regional Language Centre.

SWALES, J. M. 1990, *Genre Analysis: English in Academic and Research Settings*. Cambridge: Cambridge University Press.

TARONE, E. and YULE, G. 1989, *Focus on the Language Learner*. Oxford: Oxford University Press.

WIDDOWSON, H. 1984, Educational and pedagogic factors in syllabus design. In C. J. BRUMFIT (ed.) *General English Syllabus Design: Curriculum and Syllabus Design for the General English Classroom* (pp. 23–8). ELT Documents 118. Oxford: British Council and Pergamon Press.

—— 1987, Aspects of syllabus design. In M. L. TICKOO (ed.) *Language Syllabuses: State of the Art* (pp. 65–89). Singapore: Regional Language Centre.

—— 1990, *Aspects of Language Teaching*. Oxford: Oxford University Press.

WILKINS, D. A. 1976, *Notional Syllabuses*. Oxford: Oxford University Press.

WRIGHT, T. 1987, Instructional task and discoursal outcome in the L2 classroom. In C. N. CANDLIN and D. F. MURPHY (eds) *Language Learning Tasks* (pp. 47–68). London: Prentice-Hall International.

YALDEN, J. 1987, *Principles of Course Design for Language Teaching*. Cambridge: Cambridge University Press.

YORKEY, R. C., BARRUTIA, R., CHAMOT, A. U., DE DIAZ, I. R., GOLDMAN, L. J., GONZALEZ, J. B., HENDERSON, R. T., NEY, J. W. and WOOLF, W. L.,

1985, *New Perspectives. Intermediate English 1*. Massachusetts: Heinle and
Heinle Pub. Inc.
ZOBL, H. 1983, Markedness and the projection problem. *Language Learning* 33,
293–313.

Appendix 1

From R. C. Yorkey *et al.*, 1989, *New Perspectives. Intermediate English 1.*
Massachusetts: Heinle and Heinle Pub. Inc.

Contents

Appendix 1a

From R. C. Yorkey *et al.*, 1989, *New Perspectives. Intermediate English 1.*
Massachusetts: Heinle and Heinle Pub. Inc.

1 Vocabulary in Context

Fill in the blanks with the correct word or expression. Use each item only once.

Nouns	Verbs	Adjective	Expression
bill	keep track of	jealous	in no time
deposit	persuade		
robot	program		
withdrawal			

Charles Johnson is talking to Nancy Tanner.
CHARLES: Hey, Nancy! Guess what! My parents are going to buy me a __(1)__.
NANCY: Really?! That's great! How did you __(2)__ them to do that?
CHARLES: I told them that it would help me with my schoolwork and, of course, it'll help them, too.
NANCY: Your parents have schoolwork?
CHARLES: No, but they can use it to __(3)__ their money. Every time they pay a __(4)__ or make a __(5)__ or a __(6)__ from their bank account, all they have to do is tell the robot. There's a computer in a robot, you know.
NANCY: Wow, a computer! Just think. You can __(7)__ it to play all kinds of games, and you'll be able to do your math homework __(8)__. I'm __(9)__. I wish my parents would buy me one.
CHARLES: Why don't you ask them? Maybe they will.
NANCY: I've already asked them. No luck.

2 Focus on Grammar   Verb + object + verb (Summary A1)

In these sentences, the subject does not do the action but causes another person to do it.

1. If you buy a robot, you won't have to do housework.
   You can **have the robot do** the housework for you.
2. Kathy and Nancy don't like to do their homework, but they do it.
   Kathy and Nancy's parents **make them do** their homework.
3. Kathy and Nancy's parents say that they can go out after they finish their homework.
   They **let** Kathy and Nancy **go out** after they finish their homework.

Note: The verb *help* can take the base form of the verb or the base form with *to*.

4. Kathy's not good at math, but Nancy is.
   Nancy **helps** Kathy **do** her math.
   Nancy **helps** Kathy **to do** her math.

3 Practice

Complete each sentence by putting the words in parentheses in the correct order.

1. A robot can (Nancy/do/help) her homework.
2. Big industries often (robots/have/do) some of the work in factories.
3. Nancy's parents won't (stay/her/let) out late at night.
4. Nancy (turn off/her sister/makes) the TV while she's studying.

Appendix 2

From C. Madden and S. M. Reinhart, 1987, *Pyramids, Structurally Based Tasks for ESL Learners.* Ann Arbor, MI: The University of Michigan Press.

Contents

Appendix 2a

From C. Madden and S. M. Reinhart, 1987, *Pyramids, Structurally Based Tasks for ESL Learners.* Ann Arbor, MI: The University of Michigan Press.

Lesson 1   New Students

■ Here are some information cards for four new students in Level 2 at the English Language Academy. Some information is missing from them. Listen to the conversation and write in the missing information about the new students.

Name: _Gabriela_
Country: _Portugal_
Birth date: _8/25/50_
Married ☑
Single ☐
Occupation: _doctor_
Interests and hobbies:
reading & photography

Name: _Samuel_
Country: _____
Birth date: _2/4/65_
Married ☐
Single ☐
Occupation: _student_
Interests and hobbies:
classical music

Name: _Kuniko_
Country: _Japan_
Birth date: _____
Married ☐
Single ☐
Occupation: _____
Interests and hobbies:
volleyball & swimming

Name: _____
Country: _Morocco_
Birth date: _____
Married ☐
Single ☐
Occupation: _____
Interests and hobbies:
_____

Complete the following summary about Kuniko:

Kuniko is _____ Japan. She was born on _____. She _____ married. She _____ Japanese. She is a student and she _____ to play volleyball and swim.

• Now find out the same information about some of your classmates by interviewing each other. Complete an information card for each classmate you interview.

Appendix 3

From N. S. Prabhu, 1987, *Second Language Pedagogy*. Oxford: Oxford University Press.

TASK 1   *Task* Sheets of paper containing the following timetable and the questions below it are handed out. The teacher asks a few questions orally, based on an anticipation of learners' difficulties (for example, 'Is this a day train or a night train?' in view of the difference from the pre-task timetable, and 'For how long does the train stop at Jolarpet?' in view of students' observed difficulty in calculating time across the hour mark) and then leaves the class to do the task.

	Madras	Arkonam	Katpadi	Jolarpet	Kolar	Bangalore
Bangalore	Dep. 2140	Arr. 2250	Arr. 0005	Arr. 0155	Arr. 0340	Arr. 0550
Mail		Dep. 2305	Dep. 0015	Dep. 0210	Dep. 0350	

1 When does the Bangalore Mail leave Madras?
2 When does it arrive in Bangalore?
3 For how long does it stop at Arkonam?
4 At what time does it reach Katpadi?
5 At what time does it leave Jolarpet?
6 How long does it take to go from Madras to Arkonam?
7 How long does it take to go from Kolar to Bangalore?

Students' performance:

7 or 6 answers correct	14 students
5 or 4 answers correct	8 students
3 or 2 answers correct	6 students
1 or 0 answers correct	3 students
	31

TASK 2   The next lesson based on railway timetables presented students with the following task (following a similar pre-task) as representing an appropriate increase in complexity:

	Madras	Arkonam	Katpadi	Jolarpet	Kolar	Bangalore
Bangalore	Dep. 2140	Arr. 2255	Arr. 0005	Arr. 0155	Arr. 0340	Arr. 0550
Mail		Dep. 2305	Dep. 0015	Dep. 0210	Dep. 0350	
Bangalore	Dep. 1300	Arr. 1420	Arr. 1515	Arr. 1647	Arr. 1825	Arr. 2020
Express		Dep. 1440	Dep. 1520	Dep. 1650	Dep. 1830	
Brindavan	Dep. 0725	—	Arr. 0915	Arr. 1028	—	Arr. 1300
Express			Dep. 0920	Dep. 1030		

Questions:

1 When does the Bangalore Express arrive at Katpadi?
2 At what time does the Bangalore Mail leave Arkonam?
3 For how long does the Bangalore Express stop at Jolarpet?
4 Which trains stop at Arkonam?
5 Where is the Brindavan Express at twelve noon?
6 Where is the Bangalore Express at three p.m.?
7 Mr Ganeshan wants to travel from Madras to Kolar. He has some work in Kolar in the morning. By which train should he travel?
8 Mrs Mani has to work in Madras on the morning of Monday. She wants to get to Bangalore on Monday night. Which train can she take?

Appendix 4

From J. M. Brown and A. S. Palmer, 1988, *The Listening Approach: Methods and Materials for Applying Krashen's Input Hypothesis*. London: Longman.

Lists of Ideas

1. CLASSROOM PROCEDURES AND PROJECTS
*1. Find out students' names and make a seating chart [A]
*2. Arrange the classroom [B]
*3. Talk about who is late, and why [B]
*4. Take a break [B]
*5. Use students' names to teach the names of the letters of the alphabet [C]
*6. Have a bake sale [C/D]
*7. Have a party: celebrate a student's birthday, a holiday, the end of the term [C/D]

2. MANIPULATIONS
1. Different kinds of pencils [A]
2. Put paper on book [A]
3. Dip, measure, and pour water, with cups, glasses, spoons [B]
*4. Colored blocks [B]
5. Food storage containers [B]
*6. Clock with movable hands [B]
*7. Money: coins and bills [B/C]
8. Dolls/toy figures doing things [C]
*9. Simple mathematical operations [C]
•
•
•

*1. Morning routine: awakening, getting up, showering, eating breakfast (coffee, toast) [C]
*2. Ongoing stories [C]
*3. Bathing [C]
*4. Driving to work [C]
*5. Eating a meal [C]
*6. Washing dishes [C]
7. Doing laundry [C]
*8. Comment on homemade videotapes of routines, cooking a meal, cleaning a room, shopping for a gift with a friend [C/D]

4. DEMONSTRATIONS
*1. A toy: remote-controlled toy car, yo-yo, jacks, skip rope [C]
*2. A hobby-related item: camera [C]
*3. An innovative gadget: magnetic paper clip holder, adjustable multiple-hole paper punch, combination flashlight/keyholder, three-color automatic pencil, hand-held electronic game [C]
4. A hand-held calculator [C]
5. Fold paper (origami) [C]

5. PHYSICAL ACTIVITIES: SPORTS, EXERCISE, PHYSICAL GAMES, DANCING
Sports
*1. Darts [B]
*2. Headstand [C]
3. Shuffleboard [C]
*4. Pool or billiards [C]
5. Quoits [C]

Appendix 4a

From J. M. Brown and A. S. Palmer, 1988, *The Listening Approach: Methods and Materials for Applying Krashen's Input Hypothesis*. London: Longman.

Developed Activities

1. CLASSROOM PROCEDURES AND PROJECTS

Find Out Students' Names and Make a Seating Chart [A]. Have students write their names on slips of paper and put them on their desks. Ask your assistant to go to one student and look at the slip of paper with the student's name on it but not read the student's name aloud. Consult your class roll, read the name of the first student, and ask your assistant if that student is the one the assistant is standing next to. Continue until you locate the first student. Complete taking the roll in this manner. After checking attendance, draw a seating chart on the chalkboard and number the seats. Then, referring to your class roll, try to recall which student is sitting in each seat. Have your assistant correct you if you are wrong. Write the students' names on the seating chart.

Once you get to know the students, begin to assign them titles that are either amusing or descriptive. For example, a Mr. Redford could be referred to as "The Brother of Robert Redford;" a student who is known for his mechanical abilities might be called "The Engineer." A student who is assigned the task of telling the class when the period is almost finished could be called "Mr. Timekeeper," and one who is good at mathematics could be called "Ms. Mathematician."

Arrange the Classroom [B]. Frequently, you will be teaching in a classroom set up for other purposes. Instead of arranging the tables and chairs yourself, wait until the students arrive and then direct the assistant to arrange the chairs and tables. Ask students to help. Keep the instructions simple, and give them one at a time. Comment as each instruction is carried out: "Move it a little to the right, now back a little," and so on. (See Chapter 2 for suggestions on room arrangements.)

Talk about Who Is Late, and Why [B]. When students come in late, stop for a moment and talk about it with your assistant. Ask her the name of the student. Figure out how many minutes the student is late (review numbers and telling time). Comment on how many times the student has been late. Speculate on possible causes. (The students will probably understand enough to confirm or deny your guesses—in their native language or nonverbally.)

Take a Break [B]. At the start of the class, tell your assistant that you want to take a break halfway through the class. Move the hands of the clock to indicate when the break will begin and end. Periodically during class, ask the assistant what time it is and how long it will be until the break. At break time, tell the assistant to keep track (on the chalkboard) of when each student returns. After the break, talk about who was early, who was late, and by how many minutes.

Use Students' Names to Teach the Names of the Letters of the Alphabet [C]. When taking roll, write the students' names on the chalkboard. Ask the assistant which letter of the alphabet each name begins with. Write all the names that begin with the same letter in the same area of the chalkboard. For variety, ask your assistant to identify the last letter of each student's name. This activity can easily lead to a discussion of the alphabet: how many letters there are, which are the first and last, which comes before and after a given letter, which are the vowels and consonants, and so on.

4 Towards an Educational Framework for Teacher-led Tasks

*

RICHARD BERWICK
The University of British Columbia

Throughout the 1980s, language tasks evolved from a varied collection of instructional activities in second and foreign language classrooms to a foundation for instructional planning, i.e. task-based syllabuses (see discussions in Breen, 1987a, b; Candlin, 1987; Krahnke, 1987; Long, 1985, 1990; Nunan, 1988, 1989). Along the way, researchers have found tasks to be useful tools for studying processes of second language acquisition (Ellis, 1987; Pienemann, 1984; Tarone, 1988) and have noted the potential of certain task formats to improve the comprehensibility of language to which learners attend through negotiation of problematic task language (Gass & Varonis, 1985a, b; Hatch, 1978, 1983; Long, 1980; Porter, 1983).

Conceptual thinking about tasks in applied linguistics has been initiated but not significantly extended in studies of *interaction strategies* (examples include Færch & Kasper, 1983; Tarone, 1983; Wagner, 1983). In addition, a number of quasi-experimental studies have described contrasting sets of what may be termed candidate task constructs — categorical distinctions of potential value in building a theoretical framework for tasks — and a rationale for the application of *negotiated interaction* to second language instructional settings. Categorical distinctions which figured prominently during the 1980s include one-way/two-way tasks (Gass & Varonis, 1985a; Long, 1980), convergent/divergent tasks (Duff, 1986), optional/required information exchange tasks (Doughty & Pica, 1986; Pica, 1987), and information exchange/decision-making tasks (Pica, 1987). Other contrasting sets have been proposed in the literature in sufficient numbers to warrant a construction of research-driven task typologies, although Long (1989: 40) has pointed out that 'embryonic taxonomies of pedagogic tasks' thus far developed have largely failed to draw upon the body of the empirical research which has already been accomplished (but for notable exceptions see Brown & Yule, 1983; Pica, Kanagy & Falodun, 1993).

Inductive approaches to task description thus provide us with a starting point at which to consider the outline of a framework for the study of tasks, but they are unable to offer the kind of predictive and explanatory power which researchers or planners of instructional programs will find at the level of a theoretical framework. Although the functional rationale for tasks in second language instructional planning has been argued persuasively (Long, 1989), little work has been directed at developing and testing an educational framework for teacher–learner and learner–learner discourse within which empirical study of task and task-group interactions can be conducted. I think it may therefore be timely to consider the sources and elements of a more deductive, empirically driven formulation of tasks which are ultimately intended for pedagogical purposes — that is, a framework for the use of tasks in second and foreign language instructional environments which draws its major concepts from the mainstreams of social and educational research.

Concepts of Knowing and Doing in Applied Research

A distinction between theoretical and practical knowledge (Schwab, 1971; also Leinhardt, 1990) and explication of the processes by which forms of practical knowledge may be communicated to learners through individual and social experience (Dewey, 1956; Vygotsky, 1962; also Bruner, 1960; Hofstadter, 1962) are among the more durable themes in social research. The theoretical–practical dichotomy has been represented recently in various disciplines and expanded to studies of how language use in such everyday settings as work and school enculturates naive participants in recognizably appropriate patterns of knowledge and behavior.

Following Cicourel's (1987, 1988, 1990) studies of medical diagnostic reasoning, for example, 'experts' are said to possess knowledge which is both *declarative* (formal, discipline-based, codified) and *procedural* (situationally constrained, socially distributed, contingently negotiated), whereas 'novices' are largely limited in their pursuit of expertise to their store of formal (declarative) knowledge. Enculturation of novices entails frequent, direct contact with experts during a variety of social encounters, many of which may bear little resemblance to the formats in which knowledge may be initially communicated, such as in textbooks and through lectures. One of Cicourel's central claims is that the enculturation process depends on *socially distributed cognition,* which refers to the fact that participants in collaborative work relationships are likely to vary in the knowledge they possesss . . . and must therefore engage each other in dialogues that allow them to pool resources and negotiate their differences to accomplish their tasks . . . [T]he knowledge sources must cooperate to solve a problem because no one source has enough information to do the job. (Cicourel, 1990: 223)

Given his focus on the social bases of learning, Cicourel emphasizes that the object of study must shift from 'the cognitive properties of individuals to on-line studies of groups in natural settings' (p. 223).

Interest in the cognitive bases of language acquisition has remained the central element of second language acquisition studies which have invoked the declarative–procedural distinction (see, in particular, O'Malley & Chamot (1990) for a review of the research; also Anderson's (1980, 1982) framework for the acquisition of cognitive skills). Recent discussion of cognitive structures assumed to underline the elaboration of competence, however, has assigned a functional role to 'social encounters', if only peripherally. In one recent example, Hulstijn (1990) relates the declarative–procedural distinction to an information-processing perspective on second language acquisition. Hulstijn argues that first and second language acquisition entail 'establishment of procedural knowledge (routine procedures) through the compilation of declarative language knowledge, and the gradual tuning and restructuring of procedural knowledge . . .' (p. 32), but acknowledges the development of implicit knowledge of language forms, meanings and functions in first language learners through social contacts with caretakers and others (p. 35).

Although there is considerable overlap in the vocabulary of constructs which have been found useful in applied research, it is also apparent that a gap exists between the meanings assigned to central explanatory constructs and to the weight or importance accorded to the social bases of cognitive development. Nevertheless, although variants on the declarative–procedural theme have received little explicit discussion in the literature of task-based second language learning, a broad interest in the effects of 'practical' discourse on second language development has clearly emerged. The social and incidental dimensions of second language acquisition have been suggested by the growing number of studies which examine the interactional qualities of discourse constructed by native speaker (NS) and non-native speaker (NNS) interlocutors (see the *negotiated interaction* studies cited above). The strong empirical basis of these studies has been taken as evidence that small group tasks which require the negotiation of propositional content conveyed in a target language contribute to a second language learner's comprehension of the discourse and, perhaps, thereby to the acquisition of a second language (see, in particular, Long's (1980, 1981, 1983a, b, 1985) discussions of the relationship among NS input, NS–NNS interaction, and second language acquisition).

Views of theoretical and practical knowledge in content and language education

An alternative, *educational,* perspective on processes of second language comprehension and learning, however, would relate the use of language tasks as contexts for elicitation of learner language (see, in particular, Crookes' (1986) cross-disciplinary discussion of tasks) to verbal exchanges and other activity which lead to intended changes in knowledge or behavior. An educational orientation to task-based *research* does not begin with a preference for one task or task type over others, but does ultimately seek, as Long (1989: 37) observes in his discussion of group work and pedagogic tasks, 'to ascertain which [tasks] serve which purposes best'. Thus, a framework for tasks in language education is concerned with establishing a rational basis for people who are responsible for organizing instruction to make principled choices among content alternatives, to relate these selections to a set of 'worthwhile' ends (Peters, 1973) and to determine what methods are appropriate for effecting the choices.

In a provocative essay on the acquisition of practical knowledge in classrooms (cf. acquisition of procedural knowledge), Brown, Collins & Duguid (1989a: 33f.) propose 'authentic activity' and 'situated cognition and invention' as alterntives to decontextualized, didactic teaching in content classrooms. *Authentic activity* is a learner's direct experience with the modes of thought and action in a field of practice. Thus, for example, learners acquire the expertise of historians or mathematicians by behaving as historians or mathematicians engaged in the exploration of a problem. *Situated cognition and invention* is based on the premise that 'knowledge is situated in activity and that it is used and made sense of within specific contexts and cultures' (Brown, Collins & Duguid, 1989b: 11). The authors contend that learners who are free to work directly with objects or representations of objects during their problem solving are able to avoid use of the sort of complex algorithms typically required when contextual support is unavailable to the problem-solver.

An appealing and controversial aspect of situated cognition (Palincsar, 1989; Weinberg, 1989) is the notion of *apprenticeship* as an alternative to the kind of decontextualized instruction content area teachers frequently employ to convey their subject matter. Apprenticeship is a process of enculturation which gradually reveals the practical knowledge experts in a given field possess and make available to novices through collective work on problems of the field. Knowledge is shared through authentic activity and 'constructed from the context, social and physical, in which they are formed' (Brown, Collins & Duguid, 1989b: 12). Although the authors are not explicit on the point, apprenticeship presumably entails the construction of meaning through language (and the use of other media) during practical activity. Recalling Cicourel's ethnographic studies of how medical knowledge is tacitly and socially acquired, it appears that expertise may be conveyed effectively even when it is expressed informally and indirectly in social exchanges between novices and experts which occur outside of conventional instructional practices in a given field. During apprenticeship, then, field-specific learning may be at least as much an incidental effect of social exchange as it is a deliberate attempt of a teacher to teach a body of subject matter.

Although the point makes little allowance for the utility of generalization and abstraction in instructional discourse, it does evoke a way of thinking about subject matter instruction in North America which has been revisited frequently by educational theorists and practitioners during the past century (see Eisner, 1988; Leinhardt, 1990; Stahl & Miller, 1989). Indeed, findings from task-based second language research which suggest experiential and social bases for second language learning offer us a link between the research interests of social scientists and applied linguists. In particular, the findings provide some justification for applying broadly conceptual thinking to task-based research in order to relate its findings to educational practice.[1]

Among the conceptual systems which effectively extend the distinction between declarative and procedural knowledge to problems in language education are Cummins' (1983) and Mohan's (1986) typologies describing the communciation of knowledge in educational settings. Both typologies are dimensionally complex but emphasize, at the same time, the relationship between context and discourse (see, for example, Cummins' distinction between context-embedded and context-reduced communication, p. 120 f.).

Mohan, in addition, focuses on the classification of activities and uses of language in educational contexts which can be applied to selection of tasks for both language and content (subject matter) learning. His typology, the *Knowledge Framework* (Mohan, 1986: 35f.), is divided into general theoretical and specific practical categories of knowledge which together encompass the kinds of expertise a learner may be expected to achieve during a course of instruction. Knowledge is communicated through an activity (i.e. a task) which, Mohan notes, combines theory (background knowledge) and practice (action situations) . . . Verbal, expository learning is essential for understanding theory and symbolic knowledge, but it needs to be associated with life experience and practical knowledge. (Mohan, 1986: 45)

Thus the distinction between expository and experiential approaches to teaching and learning is, at its broadest, the difference between content expressed through theoretical discourse over knowledge which exists independently of the situation in which it is discussed (as in lectures, textbooks, classroom discussions, for example) and content expressed through practical discourse over objects which can be referred to in the communicative situation (laboratory work, demonstrations, cooperative games).

A rather general implication of this point of view is that background knowledge in itself is not enough to define competence in a given content area. To the extent that achieving competence also entails what might be termed practical exchanges with people who possess practical knowledge, language becomes a direct, tangible medium for tapping into the experience of others. Another, more specific implication is that the qualities of verbal and non-verbal interaction by which participants in tasks attempt to achieve understanding of each other's talk may be expected to vary according to the experiential characteristics of the activity in which they are engaged.

Relating the concepts to a study of task and task-group interactions

To this point the discussion has outlined several cross-disciplinary views of how practical expertise may be acquired through social experience. It has also suggested that tasks which are constructed to bring teachers and learners together in educational settings, including those intended to support second and foreign language learning, become sources for the exchange of knowledge through varying levels of theoretical and practical discourse. What has yet to be clarified, however, is the relationship of this discourse to the kinds of tasks teachers (and other planners) of language programs may choose to employ: How does the language used during enactment of a task vary with the goals which are set for it and the processes which are employed to achieve the goals?

In an experimental study which examined the language of teacher-led tasks from the theoretical–practical point of reference (Berwick, 1988), I found that the goals and degree of experientiality embodied within a task were reflected in particular forms of textual reference, various clarification and control strategies, indications of lexical uncertainty, explicit requests for information, and other forms of discourse employed by foreign language teachers and learners during dyadic interaction. I was especially interested in comparing tasks which encompassed 'educational' or 'social' goals conducted through 'expository' or 'experiential' processes. Based on repeated measures analyses of variance and *post hoc* comparisons of significant effects, I found, for example, that definitions (produced mainly by teachers) and indications of lexical uncertainty (produced mainly by learners) characterized tasks organized to achieve educational objectives through elaboration of lesson content. The task most implicated in this allocation was a lecture–discussion about the functions of a laptop computer.

Confirmation checks, referential questions, and use of exophoric ('pointing out') reference, on the other hand, were of equal use to and the most prominent verbal resources for the dyad participants when they were engaged in cooperative, face-to-face construction of a Lego toy. I argued that this second task reflected participants' achievement of social and collaborative goals through direct experience with the objects of the discourse. It produced a relatively more intensively negotiated, roundabout flow of talk than the linear, open-and-shut pattern of discourse I encountered within the expository approach to conveying educational objectives. The study summarized the most significant allocations of what were termed *repair exponents,* four of the 14 examined in the analysis of variance, to a *complementary task structure* (p. 164) which is graphically represented in Figure 1.

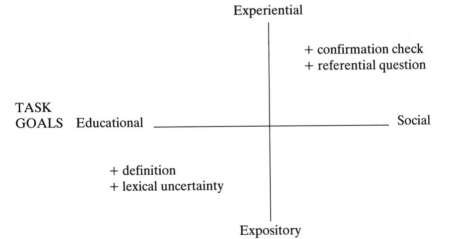

TASK PROCESSES

Experiential

+ confirmation check
+ referential question

TASK
GOALS Educational ——————————————————— Social

+ definition
+ lexical uncertainty

Expository

FIGURE 1 *Allocation of exponents to the complementary task structure by most significant effects*

The findings indicated that educational goals and expository behavior define a region or type of task which is characterized by the ways teachers and language learners talk to each other, as is the case with social (or con-ventionally negotiated) goals and experiential behavior — and that the use of certain forms of repair and reference in teacher-led groups can be schemati-cally represented within a two-dimensional structure, as is indicated in Figure 1. The Figure was intended as a convenient way of representing the allocation of coded elements of the task discourse to a way of thinking about tasks which is based on educational referents. In this sense it constitutes a rough prediction of how teacher–learner talk may be expected to materialize when tasks are selected for their orientation to goals and processes within a largely content (rather than language) based approach to selection.

Along these lines, I also suggested that categories of the complemen-tary task structure would be useful in further research, especially in extend-ing our ability to make generalizations about the relationship between task type and task language. Accordingly, in this chapter, I present a reanalysis of my earlier data with a more powerful statistical technique and attempt to refine the framework introduced initially in 1988.

Method

In what follows I will briefly describe the methods I employed in the 1988 study which form the basis for the confirmatory principal components analysis (PCA) reported in this chapter. Following Tabachnick & Fidell (1983) the confirmatory PCA was intended to 'extract the maximum vari-ance from the [1988] data set by identification of a few orthogonal com-ponents' (p. 396), that is, components which are as distinct as possible from each other, and to interpret the components with reference to a theoretical framework[2] (see 'Assignment of tasks to a conceptual framework' below).

Groups and dyads

Twelve Japanese university level learners of English as a foreign lan-guage were randomly paired with 12 university English teachers so that six of the learners were matched with native speakers of English and the remaining six were matched with native speakers of Japanese. The *mixed group* thus included six native-speaker (NS)/non-native speakers (NNS) dyads while the *homogeneous group* included six NNS–NNS dyads.

All of the Japanese teachers who participated in the study were rated by a trained interviewer at a level of 3 or higher on the 0 to 5 scale of the LPI (Language Proficiency Interview, see Educational Testing Service, 1982), evidence of a professional level of oral proficiency in English. The twelve Japanese learners of English who participated were drawn randomly from the membership list of two university English-speaking societies who scored within an intermediate range of proficiency on two tests: between 1+ and 2 on the LPI and between 65 and 80% on the CELT (Comprehensive English Language Test, see Harris & Palmer, 1986). The main purpose of selecting participants by English proficiency was to ensure that all dyads would consist of members at comparable levels, that is, a learner at an intermediate level and a teacher at native or near-native proficiency.

Tasks

The tasks used in the study included: (1) a lecture about finding character strings in a text through use of the word processing program of a laptop computer which was not physically present in the experimental setting (COM1); (2) a demonstration of how to find character strings on the laptop when it was physically present in front of the participants (COM2); (3) reconstruction of a small Lego (snap-together) toy with the participants facing away from each other, one participant relating a set of sequenced, graphic instructions as the other assembled the pieces (LEG1); (4) reconstruction of a second Lego toy with about the same number of pieces as used in LEG1 while the participants sat face-to-face (LEG2); and (5) informal discussion of any topic of common interest to the participants (DIS).

Assignment of tasks to a conceptual framework

Figure 2 outlines the assignment of tasks to the major conceptual categories of the study. An important assumption underlying the assignment, one which will be revisited in the confirmatory analysis, is that participants' orientation to goals and activities are fundamental attributes of tasks in instructional environments. COM1 and COM2 were organized around *didactic goals* in the sense that they were intended, prescriptively, to increase the learner's knowledge or competence through explicit instruction of subject matter which an educational authority (typically a teacher) considers worth learning. LEG1, LEG2, and DIS were considered tasks organized around *collaborative goals* in that they emphasized cooperative, consensual behavior and exchange of information about a problem or topic which participants explore freely during the task itself; participants structure the task contingently through their use of language and other forms of communicative behavior. (See Ellis (1984) and Malamah-Thomas (1987) for related typologies of interaction goals in second language classrooms.)

Four of the tasks were also classified according to the extent to which they seemed, prospectively, to emphasize the role of perception and activity in the operation of the task, that is, according to the extent to which they emphasized the role of *experience* over *exposition*. 'Experience' was simplified in practice to refer to whether or not dyad members could point

| | Processes: | | |
	Expository	⟵——⟶	Experiential
Goals:			
Didactic	COM1		COM2
Collaborative	LEG1	DIS	LEG2

FIGURE 2   *Goal and process dimensions of the five tasks used in the study*

out or manipulate and see things in the task environment. Thus, it was assumed that the most intense level of experiential activity would be found in LEG2 and COM2 (+doing, +seeing), a more moderate level in LEG1 (+doing, –seeing), and the lowest level in COM1 (–doing, –seeing), a task which was also designed to encourage the teacher to use didactic, lecture-like behavior in order to navigate the task.

The dependent variables

Among the large number of behaviors studied as dependent variables in recent, largely empirical, work in the area of task, group and task–group interactions (see Chaudron (1988) and Long (1989) for comprehensive reviews), frequencies for clarification requests, comprehension checks, confirmation checks, definitions, display questions, echoes, expressions of lexical uncertainty, referential questions, self-expansions, self-repetitions, other-expansions, and other-repetitions were selected for the principal components analysis. Appendix 1 lists definitions and examples of the exponents in context. The items on this list were treated as exponents of repair, defined broadly as verbal or other behavior interlocutors use to signal misunderstanding or to initiate an exchange which is intended to either forestall or repair misunderstanding when it is perceived.

In addition, measurement of the distinction between expository and experiential behavior in the dyads was operationally related to the occurrence, respectively, of anaphoric ('pointing back') or exophoric ('pointing out') reference in the spoken texts of each of the tasks (see Halliday & Hasan, 1976, 1989). Thus, it was predicted that experiential texts would be characterized by a relatively high level of exophoric (but low level of anaphoric) reference, while, it was assumed, just the reverse would be the case for the expository texts. Although the distinction between expository and experiential activity has a broad educational foundation and a strong conceptual basis in language education (Mohan, 1986), it has not yet been examined directly as a problem in factor analytic or principal components designs in second language research.

Recording and treatment of the data

In order to reduce carry-over effects, all dyads experienced the same five communication tasks in an order dictated by a standard Latin Square assignment of task order to each of the dyads in either the mixed or homogeneous groups (see Elmes, Kantowitz & Roediger, 1985; Ferguson, 1981). That is, the order of the first dyads' set of five tasks was rotated by one task for the next dyad's scheduled combination of tasks, and so on until the last dyad for the group (either NS–NNS or NNS–NNS) had worked through its scheduled tasks.

Dyad members sat face-to-face during LEG2, COM2 (and were permitted to manipulate the computer during the string-searching demonstration or point to objects during assembly of the Lego pieces), as well as during DIS (the free discussion task) and COM1 (the lecture about string searching on the laptop computer). Participants sat back-to-back during LEG1 as the teacher related the contents of the uncaptioned assembly diagram to the learner. DIS required no equipment and allowed either participant to initiate the discussion. Dyadic activity during all tasks was audio recorded for approximately seven minutes by the researcher, who sat at a remote location during the task activity. The second to seventh minutes of talk during each of 60 dyadic exchanges (five tasks × two groups × six dyads in each group) were transcribed following audio recording and then coded for all of the exponents of repair and reference. Coding reliability was estimated by training ten native speakers of English to interpret a random selection of half of the exponents in context and then obtaining recodings of a set of twenty excerpts from the transcripts from the raters. An inter-rater reliability coefficient of 0.91 (Kendall's Coefficient of Concordance W) indicated a satisfactory level of agreement on assignment of codes to the transcripts.

Table 1 summarizes all significant effects in the study for each of the exponents of repair and reference.

Design of and implementation of the confirmatory study

The 1988 study found very few significant differences between the two groups of teacher-led dyads. Consequently, the exponents of repair and reference for all of the dyads were combined in a single case-by-task data matrix for the present study. This produced, initially, 12 cases for each of the 14 exponents ($N = 168$) by all of the tasks. Five outliers were removed, leaving an N of 163.

TABLE 1   *Significant repair exponents and sources of variance for all tasks*

Repair/reference exponent	F ratio	p	Main sources of variance*	
			$p < 0.05$	$p < 0.01$
Clarification request	5.646	0.001	LEG1 > DIS LEG2 > DIS	LEG1 > DIS —
Comprehension check	11.191	0.001	LEG1 > DIS LEG1 > LEG2 LEG1 > COM2 LEG1 > COM1	LEG1 > DIS LEG1 > LEG2 LEG1 > COM2 LEG1 > COM1
Confirmation check	11.680	0.001	LEG2 > DIS LEG2 > COM2 LEG2 > COM1 LEG2 > LEG1	LEG2 > DIS LEG2 > COM2 LEG2 > COM1 —
Definition	3.434	0.017	COM1 > LEG2 COM1 > DIS	— —
Display question	23.220	0.001	COM2 > LEG1 COM2 > LEG2 COM2 > DIS COM2 > COM1 COM1 > LEG1	COM2 > LEG1 COM2 > LEG2 COM2 > DIS COM2 > COM1 COM1 > LEG1
Echo	4.455	0.005	COM2 > DIS COM1 > DIS	COM2 > DIS COM1 > DIS
Lexical uncertainty	8.016	0.001	DIS > LEG2 DIS > COM2 COM1 > LEG2 COM1 > COM2	DIS > LEG2 DIS > COM2 COM1 > LEG2 COM1 > COM2
Referential question	11.920	0.001	DIS > COM1 DIS > COM2 LEG2 > COM1 LEG2 > COM2 LEG1 > COM1 LEG1 > COM2	DIS > COM1 DIS > COM2 LEG2 > COM1 — LEG1 > COM1 —
Self-expansion	3.167	0.024	LEG2 > DIS COM2 > DIS	— COM2 > DIS

TABLE 1   *Continued*

			Main sources of variance *	
Repair/reference exponent	*F ratio*	*p*	*p < 0.05*	*p < 0.01*
Self-repetition	7.829	0.001	LEG2 > DIS COM1 > DIS	LEG2 > DIS COM1 > DIS
Anaphora	3.187	0.023	LEG1 > COM2	—
Exophora	48.108	0.001	LEG2 > LEG1 LEG2 > DIS LEG2 > COM1 LEG2 > COM2 COM2 > LEG1 COM2 > DIS COM2 > COM1	LEG2 > LEG1 LEG2 > DIS LEG2 > COM1 LEG2 > COM2 COM2 > LEG1 COM2 > DIS COM2 > COM1

* Tukey's HSD

Preliminary (unrotated) PCA of the frequencies for repair and refer-ence suggested a three-component solution, with respective eigenvalues of 3.358, 0.808, and 0.376. Although an eigenvalue of 1 is often taken as a useful point at which to limit the number of components in a final solution, a Scree test which graphed the eigenvalues showed levelling off well beyond 0.376 and suggested the inadequacy of a two-component solution (see Spearritt (1988) for further discussion). Components with eigenvalues below 0.376 were dropped from further analysis. Varimax rotation resulted in a three component solution accounting for about 91% of the total variance.[3]

Table 2 shows the elements of the analysis from initial to final solution. The table indicates that the discussion (DIS) and back-to-back Lego (LEG1) tasks together contributed a considerable amount of the 'explain-able' variance to the first component, with COM1, the lecture about string searching on laptop computers, adding a moderate contribution to the com-ponent. The second component, on the other hand, was largely a function of the two demonstration tasks, especially of LEG2 and, to a slightly lesser degree, of COM1. The two tasks which entailed instruction in the string searching function of the computer, COM1 and COM2, shared most of the variance on the third component.

TABLE 2   *Summary of the principal components analysis*

		Components		
		1	*2*	*3*
Latent roots (eigenvalues)		3.358	0.808	0.376
Rotated loadings	COM1	0.440	0.240	0.824
	COM2	0.212	0.682	0.627
	DIS	0.910	0.205	0.191
	LEG1	0.793	0.196	0.404
	LEG2	0.219	0.941	0.178
Variance explained by rotated components		1.744	1.494	1.304
Percent of total variance explained		34.889	29.881	26.076

Interpretation of the components

Graphic representation of these component loadings provides a way to relate the tasks to the framework proposed in my earlier study (and, by extension, to the theoretical–practical, declarative–procedural distinctions proposed in the non-empirical studies which support it). Figure 3 shows a three-dimensional structure with preliminary labels for the principal components. Component labeling was assisted by reference to Table 1 which indicates the relative contribution of the exponents of repair and reference to each of the tasks on the basis of a hierarchy of significant effects achieved during analysis of variance in the first study.

Component 3 has been labeled $+/-didactic$ to accommodate the distribution of tasks and talk within tasks along the z-axis. The higher or 'positive' end of the axis includes, at roughly equivalent levels, the two tasks (COM1 and COM2) which were explicitly designed to accomplish instructional goals set prior to the start of the tasks and which entailed the frequent use of definitions, display questions and echoic behavior. The remaining tasks occupy decreasing values on the axis, running from LEG1 to DIS and then to LEG2. Given the kinds of repair and reference which occurred during performance of the discussion and face-to-face Lego tasks — clarification requests, comprehension checks, and referential questions — it is possible to suggest that the 'negative' end of the axis reflects the use of language to accomplish largely collaborative and social goals through language.

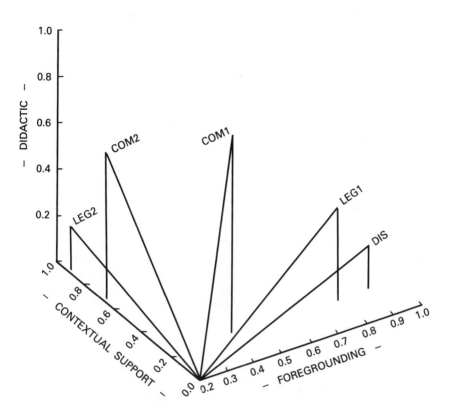

FIGURE 3   *Principal components in dimensional space*

Components 2 and 1 have been labelled, respectively, $+/-$*contextual support* and $+/-$*foregrounding* to capture the degree of experiential behavior which the various tasks appear to support. The highest level of contextual support, provided through the intensive use of exophoric reference as a means of pointing out objects in the task environment, seems most evident in LEG2 and COM2. These tasks encouraged participants to designate such objects as keys on the keyboard, letters on the computer's display, plastic pieces of various shapes and colours as literal points of reference to accompany their verbal descriptions and explanations. The remaining three tasks fall closely together at the other ('negative') end of the y-axis, suggesting a mainly bivalent aspect to task performance in the use of exophoric reference, at least, to supply contextual support: tasks either provide physical, visible contextual clues of simultaneous use to participants during the task or they do not, regardless of the other methods participants may employ to make their talk comprehensible to each other.

When contextual support in the form of exophoric reference cannot be used productively, as was the case in COM1, LEG1, and DIS, participants attempt to keep their talk comprehensible through such alternative procedures as providing textual cohesion in the form of anaphoric reference. Provision of textual cohesion through anaphora was a significant resource during the back-to-back Lego task, but also played an important role in the performance of the computer lecture and the discussion. Textual cohesion thus appears to serve as a kind of alternative to contextual support, allowing dyadic participants to keep track of the objects of their talk and to link propositions within the text together when direct, shared experience is unavailable as a task resource.

The remaining component of experiential behavior, $+/-foregrounding$ (the x-axis) reveals a clear division between two tasks which required collaborative verbal exchanges (LEG1 and DIS) and the one task which did not (COM1). Further inspection of Table 1 suggests that foregrounding for the collaborative tasks may be accomplished through the use of questions which have the effect of drawing a partner's attention to objects or candidate topics, most particularly through the use of clarification requests, comprehension checks and referential questions. In contrast to the frequent physical pointing-out which accompanies reference to objects in tasks carried out within a shared perceptual field, these kinds of questions are purely verbal moves which may not be expressly intended to direct or redirect a partner's attention. To the extent that they do have these effects, however, they may be said to serve as a complement to the use of exophoric reference in the shared-perception tasks by intensifying the flexibility with which participants survey physical or topical opportunities during work on their task.

The smallest degree of foregrounding occurs in COM1. Because this task was especially marked by definitions offered by the teacher, most frequently in connection with the learner's lexical uncertainty, it may be useful to think of requesting and making definitions as serving a 'backgrounding' function during the task. Inspection of the transcripts for this task (see the following textual analysis) suggests that a definition is perhaps the least productive approach to conveying information of use in collaborative, experience-intensive task settings, but that it is virtually a *pro forma* element of didactic, non-collaborative task behavior. Definition under these conditions provides background information to learners and opportunities for teachers to compensate for perceived or assumed gaps in learners' knowledge of the group of abstractions around which a lesson may be organized.

Various levels of contextual support and foregrounding are thus viewed here as the dimensional foundations for more or less 'experientiality' in the task discourse. Among the five tasks arrayed within these dimensions, it turns out that the least experiential, in terms of both contextual support and foregrounding, is COM1, a task most characterized by the use of definitions, echoic behavior, and lexical uncertainty. These forms of verbal activity, taken together as the most significant exponents of teacher–learner exchange during the lecture–discussion task, comprise what may be termed the central elements of an 'expository' approach to conduct of the task and thus help to define regions of decreasing experientiality in the task discourse.

Figure 4 extends the preliminary model of components developed thus far into a three dimensional model of *key task attributes,* suggests labels for the terminal points of the three dimensions, and indicates which points supplement those proposed in the first study. The unboxed attributes (*foregrounding, backgrounding, contextual support,* and *textual support*) are shown as elements of the experiential and expository task process attributes and represent the main areas in which the PCA has indicated a revision for the first study. The +/−didactic component has also been redrawn with terminal points (*didactic* and *collaborative* both revisions to the somewhat narrower terminology of the first study). In principle, any task can be located within dimensions of the model and can be described in terms of its attributes. Thus for example, it may be possible to speak of a didactic task which requires extensive use of textual support and backgrounding, or a collaborative task which relies on textual support and foregrounding.

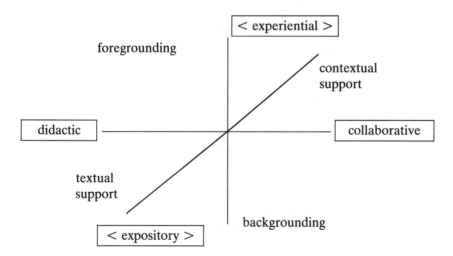

FIGURE 4   *Dimensions of task attributes in the confirmatory study*

The discourse of task attributes

One way to highlight distinctions among the attributes proposed to this point is to move directly to the dyadic talk which underlies them. The following excerpts from the task transcripts illustrate some of the essential differences by contrasting a task which contains high didactic and low experiential values (COM1) with a task which contains low didactic and high experiential values (LEG2). The teacher's talk is shown in capital letters and the learner's in lower case. Codings are bracketed in the right margin immediately following the utterance to which they refer.

Excerpt (1), from the lecture about string searching, begins with a display question designed to test cognitive knowledge. The learner's lexical uncertainty is taken as evidence that more instruction is required, which the teacher supplies immediately in the form of definitions — one following each indication of lexical uncertainty. The definitions and indications of lexical uncertainty have been italicized in the text.

1. DO YOU KNOW WHAT A – PIECE OF STRING
    IS   [DISPLAY Q.]

    String – –   [ECHO]
    /IN OTHER WORDS, THREAD?

    Thread? Ah, thread. Uh –   [LEX UNCERT.]

    THAT'S IT. A STRING IS JUST A THICK   [ANAPH]
    PIECE OF THREAD.   [DEF.]

    BUT IN COMPU – –   UH. COMPUTER

    /rib – ribbon, ribbon. No.   [LEX. UNCERT.]
    DOESN'T HAVE A RIBBON. TH – THERE'S A   [OTHER REP.]
    SPECIAL MEANING OF THE WORD STRING IN
    THE COMPUTER. *IT JUST MEANS A WORD,*   [ANAPH.]
    A PHRASE OR SENTENCE.   [DEF.]

More than any of the other tasks, COM1 was concerned with communication of abstract knowledge through a verbal medium and required frequent use of anaphoric reference as a cohesive device. The task involved the teacher in short digressions over bits of knowledge related to, but not essential for, proper operation of the computer. Although teachers occasionally elicited definitions from their learners to test knowledge, it was more typically the case that they treated lexical uncertainty, both their own and the learner's, as a kind of tripwire for production of a definition which effectively cut off further opportunity for a negotiated exchange.

Excerpt 2, on the other hand, shows the learner helping to manage the face-to-face Lego task through use of referential questions, confirmation checks, and expository reference. The learners' questions have been italicized.

2. UH, BETWEEN THE TWO SQUARE ONES + +
CAN SNAP IT ON TOP OF THE TWO
SQUARE ONES.   [SELF. EXP.]

Uh – this way?   [REF. Q./EXO]

NO. THE OTHER WAY.   [Eval.–.EXO]
/No.

The other way?   [CON C./EXO]

YEAH. OKAY. PUT IT ON TOP OF THEM   [Eval.+/EXO]

Top of them?   [CON C./EXO]

YEAH. O– ON TOP OF THE TWO SQUARE PIECES   [Eval.+]
SO THE TWO– SO YOU PUSH TO TWO SQUARE   [SELF. EXP.]

PIECES TOGETHER.

Th like this?   [REF Q./EXO]

The learner's referential questions bracket attempts (in the form of confirmation checks) to obtain explicit information about the placement and spatial relationship of pieces on the table. The learner seeks and obtains frequent evaluation about the physical structure which is under construction, not about qualities of the language used to produce the model, and in so doing participates in an intensively negotiated and frequently roundabout exchange of information. At a superficial level, this roundabout quality of the task discourse can be interpreted as evidence of the inefficiency by which language is used to accomplish task goals. At a more fundamental level, however, the exploratory, comprehension-seeking use of language during the task contrasts with the rather singleminded determination of teachers to teach when they have been oriented towards achieving didactic goals through exposition (as in COM1) and the consequent 'streamlining' effect this kind of determination has on the discourse.

Discussion and conclusion

The notion of 'complementary task structures' introduced in the first study can be examined from several perspectives based on the findings of the confirmatory study. First, the evidence suggests that tasks are indeed complex structures which contain particular patterns of attributes. For example, some tasks ostensibly intended to achieve didactic goals may well provide intensive contextual support and very little verbal foregrounding for the learner; other tasks conducted with considerable verbal foregrounding may offer virtually no contextual support and provide few opportunities to accomplish didactic goals.

Various combinations of attributes begin to suggest task types which encourage distinctive forms of verbal and non-verbal behavior and which may present quite different challenges to learners at different levels of second language development. Since we know very little about what constitutes 'difficulty' for learners negotiating their way through a task, it is going to be useful to study the relationship of task attributes — some of which have been elaborated here — to learners' perceptions of task difficulty. It is therefore not enough to characterize a task by its general orientation to either goals or processes. It will also be useful to consider a range of attributes within both of these factors when selecting or designing a task intended for second language research or instructional purposes.

Second, the confirmatory study also suggests that construction of a task typology is at least as much a conceptual problem as it is an empirical one. One begins with a general framework for the communication of knowledge in educational settings and attempts to ground the framework in studies of how learners and teachers use language to respond to the demands of various tasks. This is a process of refinement which helps to transform general categories into ones which have some potential for application to problems of research or instructional design. Figure 5 summarizes the transition from conceptual to empirical reasoning in this chapter which has played an important role in developing my understanding of educational tasks.

Reading from left to right, the figure becomes increasingly specific and indicates significant elaboration of the task attributes. For example, my first study referred to 'educational' goals and 'social' processes. The confirmatory study replaces these with more descriptively adequate terms for task goals (i.e. 'didactic' and 'collaborative') and expands the range of task processes to reflect the ways in which task participants accomplish their goals.

I also want to note the encouraging convergence of terms developed during the course of my two data-based studies with those proposed by Pica, Kanagy & Falodun (1993). Pica, Kanagy & Falodun have synthesized numerous recent studies of task to produce a typology with predictive value. Their central 'goal' and 'activity' task features are very similar to the goal and process dimensions of task which I have discussed in this chapter. The convergence suggests that we are approaching the point at which researchers

	Task attributes: goals/processes	
Knowledge base	Berwick, 1988	Confirmatory study

declarative–theoretical	→ educational
	→ expository
		→ didactic
		→ expository
		  → textual support
		  → backgrounding

procedural–practical	→ social
	→ experiential
		→ collaborative
		→ experiential
		  → contextual support
		  → foregrounding

FIGURE 5 *Increasing specificity of task attributes within the knowledge bases*

and instructional planners will be able to apply a common vocabulary to describe task types and work with comparable understandings of task dynamics. This is surely a welcome trend, one which points towards more generalizable research findings and more flexible syllabus designs.

Finally, one area that needs further attention than I have been able to afford to give it in this chapter is the argument, raised from the vantage points of various disciplines, that a learner's expertise develops through assimilation of both theoretical (or declarative) and practical (or procedural) knowledge. Although it may be possible to reason that different forms of knowledge are emphasized in different task settings, as Figure 5 indicates, it is not possible at present to answer the essentially educational question of what balance might be struck, what form the alternation ought to take, between tasks which express theoretical and practical knowledge in educational settings. Brown, Collins & Duguid (1989a, b), have dealt with the question somewhat prescriptively, arguing in effect that situated cognition and communication during authentic activity is a general remedy for an overemphasis on decontextualized, didactic teaching in applied fields. Researchers in language education may want to go beyond this level of argument in order to examine the *relationship* between theoretical and practical discourse in task settings.

Appendix 1

Definitions and examples of exponents used in the study

1. *Clarification request:* The listener indicates lack of understanding through an implied or explicit request for the speaker to expand or reformulate an utterance.

   CAN YOU FIND THAT PIECE?

   +++ *I beg your pardon?*

2. *Comprehension check:* A speaker checks whether the listener has understood the utterance.

   BUMPS IS A KIND OF SMALL, UH, LIKE A CIRCLE. – CIRCLE, 'S A LITTLE BIT ELEVATED – CIRCLE, *OKAY?*

3. *Confirmation check:* A speaker requests confirmation that the previous utterance has been heard correctly by repeating a word or phrase from the utterance and adding rising intonation.

   Where?

   UHH, ++ STARTING ON THE SECOND LINE –––.

   Second line?

4. *Definition:* A speaker states what a word or phrase means, either in response to or in anticipation of the listener's lack of comprehension; the definition typically takes the form 'A is a (type of) B'.

   THAT'S IT. *A STRING IS JUST A THICK PIECE OF THREAD*––– BUT IN, IN COMPU–––   UH,
   /rib – ribbon. ribbon. No.
   COMPUTER DOESN'T HAVE A RIBBON.

5. *Display question:* Requests the listener to demonstrate knowledge or information already possessed by the speaker and known by the listener to be possessed by the speaker. The 'display' may also take the form of a rhetorical question which is answerable by the speaker who poses it.

   APPEARING – ONE LETTER BEFORE [emph] T–H–E. SEE? – SO WHY DON'T WE KEEP– ++ *IN ORDER TO FIND ANOTHER T–H–E WHAT SSSHALL I DO?*

6. *Echo:* Exact, complete or (typically) partial repetition, with flat or falling intonation, of the preceding speaker's utterance.

MHMM. NOW PRESS THE ONE THAT GOES DOWN.

Down———

7. *Indication of lexical uncertainty:* Hesitant or tentative attempt to recall or properly employ a particular word; often characterized by repetitive production of incomplete or incorrect forms of the lexical item.

   uh, I – I– I held – I h– uh, I held – the sp– uh– –
   oratorical contest, – and I took– the management – of that contest.

8. *Referential question:* A means of eliciting information which is unknown and of interest to the speaker, and which may be possessed by the hearer. Referential questions are oriented to the topic rather than to the quality of language by which the topic is expressed.

   UM – I THINK KOCHI IS FAMOUS FOR – UH + + FIGHTING DOGS.

   Ahhh!

   UH – WHAT – WHAT DO YOU CALL THEM?

9. *Self-expansion:* Partial or complete rephrasing of one's own utterance, often occurring within the speaker's turn but possibly occurring within the speaker's next turn. (The '>' indicates the referential point for the expansion.)

   YES, THAT ONE– AND THEN – >PUT IT – ON THAT – – THE LONGER ONE. + *PUT THE SQUARE ONE ON THE LONG– LONG ONE———.*

10. *Self-repetition:* Exact, partial or semantic (equivalent) repetition of one's previous utterance within five turns of that utterance. The self-repetition frequently occurs within the speaker's own turn. (The '>' indicates the referential point for the repetition.)

    YEAH + UMMM + + LET'S JUST TRY THAT. YEAH >JUST TRY IT THERE. LET'S *JUST TRY IT THERE.* WE'LL BE CREATIVE WITH THIS THING.

11. *Other-expansion:* Partial rephrasing of the previous speaker's utterance. Rephrasing typically includes new material in addition to the repetition. (The '>' indicates the referential point for the expansion.)

    I SEE IT ON PEOPLE'S FRONT DOORS OR ON THEIR CAR.
                                          /Yes, we put on cars
    OR ON THE FRONT OF THE CAR. IS IT FOR >GOOD LUCK FOR
    /Ah

THE NEW YEAR FOR THE ++ DRIVING, OR
/yes

Yeah. It means the *celebration or good luck*. Um, I think

12. *Other-repetition:* Exact, partial or semantic repetition of the previous speaker's utterance within five turns of the utterance. (The '>' indicates the referential point for the repetition.)

Uh, not inside. So, in front of the> gate.

UH HUH. I SEE, *GATE*. YOU SAID GATE. UM HM.

13. *Anaphoric reference:* Anaphoric reference points back to something concretely identified at a previous point in the text. Anaphora typically takes the form of a pronoun (thus, >BOOK . . . *IT*). *IT* cannot be interpreted without identification of the referential source ('>').

SO. ARE ALL OF THE >PIECES TURNED RIGHT SIDE UP? (/Mhmm./)

Yes, yes *they* are.

14. *Exophoric reference:* Exophoric reference points out objects or relationships in the conversational context. It is entirely context-bound and ordinarily cannot be interpreted without shared perception or experience. The text does not show a prior concrete referent for an exophoric pronoun.

TO THE RIGHT. ++ YEAH! AND DOWN! ONE– ONE---- YEAH, DOWN! BEAUTIFUL!

Ah!

THAT'S [emph] THE ONE I WANT.

Notes

1. Bernard Mohan (personal communication) has suggested that one benefit of this would be to explicitly extend the range of data from tasks in the language classroom only to tasks in every classroom.
2. Although principal factor analysis is a useful alternative to PCA, it is frequently employed as a follow-up procedure once PCA has determined the 'nature and number of common factors' (Tabachnick & Fidell, 1983: 397), two of the goals of this study. Factor analysis, moreover, has been shown to produce different factor loadings for the same correlation matrix depending on the statistical package used, regardless of rotation method, whereas PCA produces only one solution for a given matrix (Wilkinson, 1988). The follow-up factor analysis I conducted on the data set for this study produced similar solutions and similar, although somewhat exaggerated, graphic representations compared to those produced by the

PCA — results in conformity with Wilkinson's (1988) general claim that 'principal component and common factor solutions for real data rarely differ enough to matter' (p. 409).

3. In order to improve the interpretability of the components, I used varimax rotation, one of the most 'satisfactory' forms of orthogonal rotation (Spearritt, 1988: 651) and the most commonly used rotational technique (Tabachnick & Fidell, 1983). Varimax rotation increases the contrast between the maximum and minimum loadings within each component but does not distort the relationship between components.

References

ANDERSON, J. R. 1980, *Cognitive Psychology and its Implications*. San Francisco: Freeman.

—— 1982, Acquisition of cognitive skill. *Psychological Review* 89, 369–406.

BERWICK, R. F. 1988, The effect of task variation in teacher-led groups on repair of English as a foreign language. EdD thesis, University of British Columbia.

BREEN, M. 1987a, Contemporary paradigms in syllabus design: Part I. *Language Teaching* April, 81–92.

—— 1987b, Contemporary paradigms in syllabus design: Part II. *Language Teaching* July, 157–74.

BROWN, G. and YULE, G. 1983, *Teaching the Spoken Language: An Approach Based on the Analysis of Conversational English*. Cambridge: Cambridge University Press.

BROWN, J. S., COLLINS, A. and DUGUID, P. 1989a, Situated cognition and the culture of learning. *Educational Researcher* 18, 1, 32–42.

—— 1989b, Debating the situation: A rejoinder to Palincsar and Weinberg. *Educational Researcher* 18, 4, 10–12.

BRUNER, J. 1960, *The Process of Education*. Cambridge, MA: Harvard University Press.

CANDLIN, C. N. 1987, Towards task-based language learning. In C. N. CANDLIN, and D. F. MURPHY (eds) *Lancaster Practical Papers in English Language Education 7* (pp. 5–22). Englewood Cliffs, NJ: Prentice-Hall.

CHAUDRON, C. 1988, *Second Language Classrooms: Research on Teaching and Learning*. Cambridge: Cambridge University Press.

CICOUREL, A. V. 1987, The interpenetration of communicative contexts: Examples from medical encounters. *Social Psychology Quarterly* 50, 217–26.

—— 1988, Aspects of formal and tacit distributed knowledge in the collaborative organization of medical diagnostic reasoning. Paper presented at the Workshop of Technology and Cooperative Work, University of Arizona, Tucson, Arizona, February 26–28.

—— 1990, The integration of distributed knowledge in collaborative medical diagnosis. In J. GALEGHER, R. KRAUT and C. EGIDO (eds) *Intellectual Teamwork: Social and Technological Foundations of Cooperative Work* (pp. 221–42). Hillsdale, NJ: Lawrence Erlbaum Associates.

CROOKES, G. 1986, *Task Classification: A Cross-Disciplinary Review* (Tech. Rep. No. 4). University of Hawai'i Social Science Research Institute, Center for Second Language Classroom Research, University of Hawai'i at Mānoa.

CUMMINS, J. 1983, Language proficiency and academic achievement. In J. OLLER (ed.) *Issues in Language Testing Research* (pp. 108–29). Rowley, MA: Newbury House.
DEWEY, J. 1956, *The Child and the Curriculum/The School and Society*. Chicago, IL: University of Chicago Press.
DOUGHTY, C. and PICA, T. 1986, 'Information gap' tasks: Do they facilitate second language acquisition? *TESOL Quarterly* 20, 305–25.
DUFF, P. A. 1986, Another look at interlanguage talk: Taking task to task. In R. R. DAY (ed.) *Talking to Learn: Conversations in Second Language Acquisition* (pp. 147–81). Rowley, MA: Newbury House.
Educational Testing Service 1982, *ETS Oral Proficiency Testing Manual*. Princeton, NJ: Educational Testing Service.
EISNER, E. W. 1988, The primacy of experience and the politics of method. *Educational Researcher* 17, 5, 15–20.
ELLIS, R. 1984, *Classroom Second Language Development*. Oxford: Oxford University Press.
—— 1987, Interlanguage variability in narrative discourse: Style shifting in the use of the present tense. *Studies in Second Language Acquisition* 9, 1–20.
ELMES, D. G., KANTOWITZ, B. H. and ROEDIGER, H. L. 1985, *Research Methods in Psychology*. St. Paul, MN: West Publishing Company.
FÆRCH, C. A. and KASPER, R. 1983, Plans and strategies in foreign language communication. In C. FÆRCH and G. KASPER (eds) *Strategies in Interlanguage Communication* (pp. 20–60). London: Longman.
FERGUSON, G. A. 1981, *Statistical Analysis in Psychology and Education* (3rd edn). Tokyo: McGraw-Hill.
GASS, S. M. and VARONIS, E. M. 1985a, Variation in native speaker speech modification to non-native speakers. *Studies in Second Language Acquisition* 7, 37–57.
—— 1985b, Task variation and nonnative/nonnative negotiation of meaning. In S. M. GASS and C. G. MADDEN (eds) *Input in Second Language Acquisition* (pp. 149–61). Rowley, MA: Newbury House.
HALLIDAY, M. A. K. and HASAN, R. 1976, *Cohesion in English*. London: Longman.
—— 1989, *Language, Context, and Text: Aspects of Language in a Social–Semiotic Perspective*. Oxford: Oxford University Press.
HARRIS, D. P. and PALMER, L. A. 1986, *CELT Examiner's Instructions and Technical Manual*. New York: McGraw-Hill.
HATCH, E. M. 1978, Discourse analysis and second language acquisition. In E. M. HATCH (ed.) *Second Language Acquisition: A Book of Readings* (pp. 401–35). Rowley, MA: Newbury House.
—— 1983, *Psycholinguistics: A Second Language Perspective*. Rowley, MA: Newbury House.
HOFSTADTER, R. 1962, *Anti-intellectualism in American Life*. New York: Vintage.
HULSTIJN, J. H. 1990, A comparison between the information processing and the analysis/control approaches to language learning. *Applied Linguistics* 11, 30–45.
KRAHNKE, K. 1987, *Approaches to Syllabus Design for Foreign Language Teaching*. Englewood Cliffs, NJ: Prentice-Hall.
LEINHARDT, G. 1990, Capturing craft knowledge in teaching. *Educational Researcher* 19, 2, 18–25.
LONG, M. H. 1980, Input, interaction, and second language acquisition. PhD thesis, University of California at Los Angeles.

—— 1981, Input, interaction, and second language acquisition. In H. WINITZ (ed.) *Native Language and Foreign Language Acquisition: Annals of the New York Academy of Sciences, Volume 379* (pp. 259–78). New York: The New York Academy of Sciences.

—— 1983a, Linguistic and conversational adjustments to non-native speakers. *Studies in Second Language Acquisition* 5, 177–93.

—— 1983b, Native speaker/non-native speaker conversation and the negotiation of comprehensible input. *Applied Linguistics* 4, 126–41.

—— 1985, A role for instruction in second language acquisition: Task-based language teaching. In K. HYLTENSTAM and M. PIENEMANN (eds) *Modelling and Assessing Second Language Development* (pp. 77–99). San Diego: College Hill Press.

—— 1989, Task, group, and task-group interactions. In S. ANIVAN (ed.) *Language Teaching Methodology for the Nineties* (pp. 31–50). Singapore: SEAMEO Regional Language Centre.

—— 1990, Three approaches to task-based syllabus design. Paper presented at the annual TESOL Conference, San Francisco, March.

MALAMAH-THOMAS, A. 1987, *Classroom Interaction*. Oxford: Oxford University Press.

MOHAN, B. 1986, *Language and Content*. Reading, MA: Addison-Wesley.

NUNAN, D. 1988, *Syllabus Design*. Oxford: Oxford University Press.

—— 1989, *Designing Tasks for the Communicative Classroom*. Cambridge: Cambridge University Press.

O'MALLEY, J. M. and CHAMOT, A. U. 1990, *Learning Strategies in Second Language Acquisition*. Cambridge: Cambridge University Press.

PALINCSAR, A. S. 1989, Less charted waters. *Educational Researcher* 18, 4, 5–7.

PETERS, R. S. 1973, *Authority, Responsibility and Education*. London: George Allen and Unwin.

PICA, T. 1987, Second-language acquisition, social interaction, and the classroom. *Applied Linguistics* 8, 3–21.

PICA, T., KANAGY, R. and FALODUN, J. 1993, Choosing and using communication tasks for second language instruction and research. In G. CROOKES and S. GASS (eds) *Tasks in Language Learning: Integrating Theory and Practice*. Clevedon: Multilingual Matters.

PIENEMANN, M. 1984, Psychological constraints on the teachability of languages. *Studies in Second Language Acquisition* 6, 186–214.

PORTER, P. A. 1983, Variations in the conversations of adult learners of English as a function of the proficiency level of the participants. PhD thesis, Stanford University.

SCHWAB, J. J. 1971, The practical: Arts of eclectic. *School Review* 79, 75–95.

SPEARRITT, D. 1988, Factor analysis. In J. P. KEEVES (ed.) *Educational Research, Methodology, and Measurement: An International Handbook* (pp. 644–54). Oxford: Pergamon.

STAHL, S. A. and MILLER, P. D. 1989, Whole language and language experience approaches for beginning reading: A quantitative research synthesis. *Review of Educational Research* 59, 87–116.

TABACHNICK, B. G. and FIDELL, L. S. 1983. *Multivariate Statistics*. New York: Harper & Row.

TARONE, E. 1983, Some thoughts on the notion of 'communication strategy'. In C. FÆRCH and G. KASPER (eds) *Strategies in Interlanguage Communication* (pp. 20–60). London: Longman.

—— 1988, Task-related variation in interlanguage: The case of articles. *Language Learning* 38, 21–44.

VYGOTSKY, L. S. 1962, *Thought and Language.* Cambridge, MA: The MIT Press.

WAGNER, J. 1983, Dann du tagen eineeee-weisse Platte — An analysis of inter-language communication instructions. In C. FÆRCH and G. KASPER (eds) *Strategies in Interlanguage Communication* (pp. 20–60). London: Longman.

WEINBERG, S. S. 1989, Remembrance of theories past. *Educational Researcher* 18, 4, 7–10.

WILKINSON, L. 1988, *SYSTAT: The System for Statistics.* Evanston, IL: SYSTAT, Inc.

5 Critical Episodes: Reference Points for Analyzing a Task in Action

VIRGINIA SAMUDA
Sonoma State University
PATRICIA L. ROUNDS
University of Oregon

Introduction

This is an attempt to look in detail at what happens when language learners do tasks in the language classroom. The study we describe originally grew from an interest in differentiating among tasks to find if it is possible to account for what it is that makes one task 'easier' than another and what it is that makes some learners more 'successful' at task completion than others. In doing this, we had hoped to establish a set of guidelines that could assist teachers and learners in task sequencing, selection and evaluation, in terms that would make sense to them. This chapter is a preliminary step in that direction.

Issues in task complexity have been discussed from both theoretical and pedagogical standpoints (Long, 1985; Crookes, 1986). With specific reference to the selection and sequencing of tasks, Crookes argues that it should be possible to identify those characteristics of an individual task that would make it appropriate for particular learners at particular points in time. As a move towards this end, we chose to examine in detail one type of task: spot the difference (henceforth STD) because it is widely used in classrooms and also because it has been widely discussed in the second language acquisition literature. Rather than start from the structure of the task, we decided to look at the *task in action* and examine what kinds of interactional demands it placed on participants, and from this derive features by which the task could be analyzed.

Design of the Study

The present analysis is based on videotapes of four groups of four —
two native speaker (NS) groups and two non-native-speaker (NNS) groups,
attempting to complete the same STD task. Two of the groups were adult
language learners enrolled at the intermediate level of the intensive English
program at the University of Oregon American English Institute. One
group consisted of a woman who was Indonesian and three men, an Arab,
a Brazilian and an Indonesian; the other group consisted of four Japanese,
one man and three women. Prior to the recording, they were familiar with
each other because they had been in class together an average of four hours
a day for three weeks. They had frequently participated in group work and
task-based activities as a routine part of their classes, although this was the
first time they had participated in a STD task.

The other two groups were made up of native speakers of English, students enrolled at the University of Oregon. One group consisted of three
women and one man, and the other consisted of one woman and three men.
They were classmates in a Linguistics Department class, but had had little
classroom contact with each other apart from the interaction of discussion
sections and large lectures. We included data from NSs because we were
interested in collecting base-line data, that is, identifying the kinds of linguistic and interactional demands a STD task placed on the participants
independent of language competence, and in examining the effect of differing language proficiencies on the eventual outcome of the task.

We chose to use a STD task because it was a common classroom activity
for the language learners at this level. For this reason we felt fairly sure that
the discourse produced by the students would be representative of one style
of classroom-situated competence, rather than a possibly different style
which might be produced under the situational variables introduced by the
rigors of experimental conditions (Tarone, 1988). This particular STD task
required the participants to find eight differences distributed to the four
individuals. The only instructions given were that they should identify the
differences without looking at each other's pictures and without keeping a
written record of the differences as they found them.

The entire interaction was transcribed for each group to provide a sense
of overall task development. For this chapter, however, we take as a starting
point for our analysis the segments of the task in which a difference is being
discussed. The identification of each difference must be successfully accomplished to achieve overall success in the task. Hence, each time a difference
is discussed, it can be considered a potential *critical episode* which we as
analysts can predict will be shared by NSs and NNSs alike. Each critical

episode thus serves as an isolable reference point for comparison of performance across the four groups. The beginning of each critical episode was defined as the point at which a participant nominated an item that was a difference; the end was defined as the point at which they moved on to another part of the picture. The episode was considered 'successful' if the participants agreed that they had found a difference, and 'unsuccessful' if they failed to realize they had a difference.

Examination of the Data

Categorization of critical episodes

There were 40 critical episodes in these data: 30 successful episodes and 10 unsuccessful episodes. The existence of unsuccessful episodes prompted us to examine why some differences were not identified immediately by the students. We found that the differences were managed differently by the four groups, leading us to categorize them into three types.

Type 1: Absence of feature

A Type 1 difference is defined as a difference that results from the complete removal of an item from the original picture. Figure 1a gives an example of a Type 1 difference. In the original picture on the left, the man speaking on the telephone wore glasses; the difference was the result of the removal of the glasses.

Type 2: Perceptual ambiguity

A Type 2 difference is defined as a difference which causes the picture to be perceptually ambiguous because of the way an item has been deleted. Figure 1b gives an example of a Type 2 difference. On the left is the original picture; the removal of the pencil caused the picture to become ambiguous. For example, one student assumed there was a pencil because of the configuration of the hands; another student interpreted the crease in the elbow of the woman's dress as constituting a bent pencil.

Type 3: Feature absence compounded to perceptual ambiguity through lexical dysfluency

This type of difference was one which originally was designed to be a Type 1 difference, but which became more like Type 2 because of a lexical dysfluency on the part of the NNSs. Figure 1c is an example of this type of difference. The picture on the left is the original; the difference we intended was the absence of the polka dots as represented by the picture on the right. However, because the lexical item *polka dots* or *dots* or *spots* was not accessible to the NNS students, the discussion around this difference

a. *Type 1: Feature absence*

b. *Type 2: Perceptual ambiguity*

c. *Type 3: Feature absence compounded to perceptual ambiguity through lexical dysfluency*

FIGURE 1   *Spot the dfference tasks*

Excerpted from: R. E. Hill in *Line by Line,* Book Two (1983) Molinsky, S. J. & Bliss, B. Englewood Cliffs, NJ: Prentice-Hall, p. 24.

caused perceptual ambiguities for these participants, as we discuss in the next section. For the NS groups this type of difference was treated as Type 1.

If we define success on this task as finding all eight differences, only one group was successful, and this was a NS group that completed the task within 15 minutes. Each of the other groups did not find one of the differences in spite of spending approximately one hour each on the task.

Description of the discourse

From an instructional perspective, the point of tasks like STD is to provide opportunities for the learners to engage in interaction, including task management, metalanguage, and negotiation of meaning. The number of turns generated per group (Table 1) serves as a broad indicator of the substantial amount of overall interaction and the number of opportunities each individual potentially had to speak.

TABLE 1   *Number of turns generated per group*

Group	Total number of turns
NNS1	1,550
NNS2	1,567
NS1	566
NS2	1,045

Even though the critical episodes accounted for only a range of 8–15% of the turns taken, we believe this is a portion of the interaction which provides a starting place for analysis of the interactional patterns and linguistic behaviors of the learners performing this task. By examining more closely the discourse of the critical episodes, we may determine how the three types of differences elicit different language performance.

For example, Type 1 differences led to a predictable and routinized series of turns which were similar across both NS and NNS groups. Consider the following excerpt from an NS group in which NSs 1, 2, and 4 had the same picture, and NS3 had a different picture. (Note: The term 'pronouncement' is used to denote a point at which a difference has initially been identified by one of the participants. The vertical bars indicate simultaneous speech.)

Critical episode 1
a. **NS1:** does he have glasses?   (Critical Episode Topic Nomination)
b. **NS2:** yes   (Response)
c. **NS4:** yes   (Response)
d. **NS3:** no   (Response)
e. **NS4:** okay |there's one| difference (Pronouncement)
f. **NS2:** |oh, goody |
g. **NS3:** one difference...no glasses   (Pronouncement confirmation)
h. **NS4:** Jones doesn't have uh glasses
       ...okay   (Pronouncement confirmation)

Here we have a point in the interaction, line (a), at which one of the participants nominates a feature as a possible difference, and the 'glasses' actually
represent one of the differential features. In lines (b), (c), and (d) the other
participants indicate they have checked that feature and respond appro-
priately. In this case, the negative response is immediately accepted and is
followed by a pronouncement that, indeed, a difference has been established.
The two following pronouncements confirm that everyone agrees, and
serves to fix that difference in group memory since they were not allowed to
write anything.

A NNS group showed a great deal of similarity in establishing this same
difference:

Critical episode 2
a. **NNS2:** and he got...he got glasses (Critical Episode Topic Nomination)
b. **NNS4:** |yes|, but...   (Response)
c. **NNS1:** |yeah| (Response)
d. **NNS3:** |no| (Response)
e. **NNS2:** NO?   (Confirmation check)
f. **NNS4:** no?   (Confirmation check)
g. **NNS3:** huh?   (Clarification request)
h. **NNS2:** yeah, glasses   (Pronouncement)
i. **NNS3:** |ahhh |
j. **NNS1:** |glasses| (Pronouncement)
k. **NNS2:** glasses?   (Confirmation check)
l. **NNS4:** glasses, uh...   (Pronouncement confirmation)

As in the previous episode, there is a critical episode topic nomination
(line a), a response series (including a negative, thus making this a critical
episode), and finally a pronouncement series. In this case the pronouncement consists of a repetition of the topic 'glasses' four times with progres-
sively rising intonation through line (k), with normal declarative intonation
in line (l) concluding the episode. Type 1 differences were easily identified by

the participants and the critical episodes were of relatively short duration especially in clause length. In all groups, this was the first type of difference successfully negotiated, again suggesting that these differences were easier for the group participants to manage.

On the other hand, Type 2 differences (perceptual ambiguity), which depend on the individual holding the paper with the difference to make the appropriate visual interpretation of the difference, apparently provide a potential forum for more elaborate and lengthy negotiation. For example, consider the following episode from one of the NS groups. The group has already discussed the pencil (or absence thereof) and speaker NS2, holding the difference, has said she had a pencil. At the point of this excerpt, she is describing the pencil:

Critical episode 3

a.	**NS2:** |her...|...pen seems to be bent a little	(Topic nomination)
b.	**NS1:** (softly) oh	(Response)
c.	**NS3:** bent? bent?	(Clarification request)
d.	**NS4:** it's not straight?	(Clarification request)
e.	**NS2:** it's not straight...I mean... the pen that she's holding in her hand...is...is...it has a curve to it	(Clarification)
f.	**NS3:** mine doesn't	(Response)
g.	**NS1:** |mine doesn't|	(Response)
h.	**NS4:** |mine doesn't|...okay	(Response) (Pronouncement)

The group has established that three of them have straight pencils, but speaker 2's pencil is bent. Both speaker 3 and speaker 4 focus on the difference nominated, but ask for a clarification, i.e. 'bent? bent?', 'it's not straight?'. The discourse is more complex than in the previous two excerpts because of the two clarification requests and the given clarification. It is also more elaborate in terms of the variety of synonymous expressions used to describe the pencil:

'her pencil seems to be bent a little'

'it's not straight'

'it has a curve to it'

Also the speaker holding the difference appears to need to establish without a doubt that they are all talking about the same pencil, and does this by using an adjective clause, i.e. 'the pencil that she's holding in her hand ...'.

However, one of the NNS groups has a different type of difficulty with this Type 2 difference. They return to the difference in two separate critical episodes. In the first one, speaker NNS1, who has the difference, seems to agree tacitly that she has a pencil in her picture, and thus the group has an unsuccessful critical episode.

Critical episode 4
a. **NNS2:** some person | |
b. **NNS4:** |writing| a paper   (Topic nomination)
c. **NNS1:** uh huh   (Response)
d. **NNS4:** with the right hand   (Topic nomination)
e. **NNS3:** right hand?   (Clarification request)
f. **NNS1:** yes   (Clarification)

Speaker NNS1, with the difference, has had four turns to respond, but does not, even when attention is drawn to the area a second time. However, 56 pages of transcript later, this group returns to that same area of the picture. At the point from which this next excerpt is taken, 38 turns have elapsed since the renomination of the pencil as a topic, and, finally speaker NNS1 responds:

Critical episode 5
a. **NNS1:** no, no, she doesn't have a pencil
b. **NNS4:** she doesn't have a pencil?
c. **NNS1:** she |doesn't|
d. **NNS3:**\ |she | =
e. **NNS4:**   = how do you know she's writing?
f. **NNS1:** well, uh is look like…I
    mean you can tell from her |fingers |
g. **NNS4:** |okay well another difference, okay

In this excerpt, there is a second type of elaborated interaction. Beginning with line (a) speaker NNS1 states that there is no pencil in her picture, leading speaker NNS4 to challenge first her negative response, and second the previous statement that the person in the picture was writing.

Hence, there are two attested interpretations of the missing pencil: one participant sees the crease in the sleeve of the woman's dress as a pencil; another participant assumes that since the woman appears to be writing — because of the way she is holding her hand — she must be holding a writing instrument.

Finally, Type 3 differences were differences which proved to be difficult to establish for the NNSs, but not for the NSs. In the case of this STD there appeared to be one difference of this type, seemingly caused in both NNS groups by their lack of the crucial lexical item, 'polka dot'. As seen in critical episode 6 below, identifying the polka dot tie as constituting a difference is straightforward for the NSs:

Critical episode 6
a. **NS3:** |is the man| with the afro wearing a polka dot tie?
b. **NS2:** yes
c. **NS1:** |yes| | |
d. **NS4:** |NO | |he has just a...| okay there's...| |
e. **NS2:** | you| have polka dots?
f. **NS1:** yeah, polka dots
g. **NS3:** you don't
h. **NS4:** I don't have a polka |dot tie|
i. **NS2:** |okay so| we found two of yours?

The NNSs, however, have a bit more difficulty since they do not have recourse to the appropriate lexical item, as we see in the following excerpt:

Critical episode 7
a. **NNS4:** he has uh...uh...what shall I say...|neck|...tie
b. **NNS1:** |tie|
c. **NNS4:** and the tie has uh...
d. **NNS2:** little...|little| circle... |little circle|
e. **NNS4:**   little| |little circle| yeah yeah...uh

f. **NNS1:** yeah

Although speaker NNS1 has the difference she appears to agree with the rest of the group in line f, and they go on to nominate other possible differences.

As already noted, we believe that the difficulty with this difference is that it requires a lexical item like *polka dot* or *spot*. This difficulty is compounded by speaker NNS2, who substitutes 'little circle' for 'polka dot'. Speaker NNS1, attempting to match speaker NNS2's output with her picture, identifies the knot in the tie as the 'little circle'. This is one critical episode in which a lexical deficit clearly affected the eventual outcome of the task, since it posed no problem for the NSs, but both NNS groups failed to establish the polka dot tie as a difference.

In terms of discourse production, Type 2 differences placed linguistic and interactional demands on the participants which were in clear contrast to the straightforward elliptical interactions evidenced in Type 1 and Type 3 differences. Since the speakers have to go beyond the narrow confines of the routinized discourse to resolve the critical episode, Type 2 differences provide a site for enhanced L2 performance. In addition to the qualitative difference discussed above, the figures in Table 2 provide quantitative indication that Type 2 differences are the foci of comparatively extended interaction.

TABLE 2   *Average number of turns and words per types of difference*

	Number of CE	Average turns per episode	Average words per episode
Type 1	19	10	34
Type 2	15	16	71
Type 3	6	12	42

Type 2 differences result in more turns per episode and nearly twice as many words per episode on the average for all groups.

Discussion

From an SLA perspective, it seems that Type 2 differences offer more opportunity for language performance, and thus, acquisition potential, than Types 1 or 3, if we accept Swain's (1985) proposal that acquisition may be enhanced in contexts where learners are 'pushed' to convey messages 'precisely'. Trying to explain the difference between, for example, what one is seeing in the 'bent pen' example appears to require more precision in description, e.g. the use of a series of synonymous expressions, than simply establishing the presence or absence of the man's (undescribed) glasses.

Certain classroom implications may be drawn from an understanding of these differences. First, in the context of STD tasks, the distinction between Type 1 and Type 2 differences could be exploited in task design to help learners work at their own pace through the task. For example, in a class of varying proficiency levels, different versions of the same task (i.e. find the eight differences in these pictures) could be given to all students, but the differences could be 'graded' to match the proficiency levels of different groups of students. The strongest students could be given more Type 2 differences; the weaker students could be given more Type 1 differences to ensure a degree of success in task completion. This kind of grading of task enables teachers to establish an overall shared context for the task, while responding to individual differences among learners in a class.

Second, the Type 1/Type 2 distinction can help teachers set tasks which are appropriate for the developing needs of their students. For example, for many students working in small groups is an unfamiliar and threatening experience (Carter, Legutke & Thomas, 1987; Bassano, 1986). In such cases a teacher will want to sensitize them to a different mode of working, and to help them work productively and comfortably together. One way of doing this is to use a task with only Type 1 differences, which by being 'easier' will promote a sense of achievement and satisfaction among the learners, and assist in motivating them in future group work. Further, in the context of an 'easy' task learners can be directed to pay attention to meta-discoursal skills, such as techniques for monitoring input.

Critical Episodes in Action

An outgrowth of this study is the identification of critical episodes as a site for enhanced L2 performance. As opposed to an activity such as free discussion, which relies on participants' voluntary interest to go on, tasks with critical episodes provide hurdles that the participants must negotiate in order to achieve some measurable success.

The concept of critical episodes is also useful as a research construct. Designing tasks with critical episodes provides a starting point for analysis, an isolable reference point for comparison of L2 performance across groups. For example, Yule & Macdonald (1990) utilized this concept in analyzing the effect of proficiency and interactive role in pair work.

We conclude with one more way in which we feel the notion of critical episodes in task can serve both teachers, students and analysts. Consider this exchange from the data:

Critical episode 8
a. **NNS1:** with a tie
b. **NNS4:** uh huh
c. **NNS1:** the tie is like...small dots
d. **NNS4:** uh huh

In this episode, speaker NNS4's picture did not have dots on the tie, yet he responded as if it did. The inappropriateness of this response within the context of a critical episode helped us, as teachers, to isolate potential sites for instruction through post-performance feedback. First of all, the student needed to focus on strategic competence, i.e. even though keeping the channels of communication open is a good overall strategy, in this context it is inappropriate if there is any doubt of the interlocutor's meaning. Secondly, since designing a task to include critical episodes ensures that all the learners will have shared similar episodes in completing the task, teachers are guaranteed a uniform context for feedback.

This exchange (which is typical of most in the data) also suggests that, in the context of the SLA literature, we need to look again at the notion of 'appropriate response'. Long (1980) characterizes input as comprehensible if an appropriate response is made. However, Hawkins (1985) showed by means of retrospective interviews that what appears to be an appropriate response to a listener does not necessarily signal comprehension of what the speaker intended. We believe that the concept of 'critical episodes' furthers the analytic avenues adopted by Hawkins. Because the interactional response is predetermined in critical episodes, analyzing the learners' inter-actions at these points enables researchers and teachers to sift out the apparently appropriate responses that do not signal comprehension from those that do. That is, we can distinguish 'goal-appropriate responses' from 'appropriate responses'.

Interactions such as this, when viewed in the context of critical epi-sodes, assist language teaching specialists in further refining the notion of 'shared incompetence' (Varonis & Gass, 1985) among NNSs who are of approximately the same test-defined proficiency level. Speaker NNS4's inappropriate response can indicate for us a point at which a check is needed yet not requested. Therefore, it appears that a picture of NNSs participating freely because of a sense of 'shared incompetence' across the group is more complicated than it might seem on the surface. Post-task interviewing of the interactants may help us understand how differential group competences evolve (Rounds, 1985, 1987).

Conclusions

It has been argued (Crookes & Rulon, 1986) that the nature of a STD task is such that it may motivate only a very impoverished linguistic environ-ment. This study indicates that if all the differences are of Type 1, this obser-vation may be justified. However, as we have shown, a judicious use of Type 2 differences can ensure more elaborate and lengthy negotiation, and can thereby maximize the L2 performance and acquisition potential of a STD task.

From a curriculum design perspective, the distinction between Type 1 and Type 2 differences enables us to grade and sequence tasks according to difficulty, i.e. a STD which has only Type 1 differences is by definition an easier task than one which includes Type 2 differences. This is evidenced by the fact that NSs also have more difficulty in negotiating Type 2 differences than Type 1. Therefore, we contend that comparison across NS and NNSs is essential in determining the acquisition potential and the inherent difficulty of tasks.

In this study, we have tried to make a case for approaching task research in a way that we believe is sensitive to the complex of variables that come into play when groups of learners come together to collaborate on tasks. In particular, we have tried to present an analytic approach that takes account of the development of discourse *vis à vis* the goals of a task. Such an approach has led us to identify the analytic construct 'critical episodes'. At the same time, we also recognize that trying to account for differences among tasks without taking into account the perspectives of the participants involved gives only a partial and somewhat limited picture of the whole (Rounds, 1987; Samuda, 1990). However, we contend that the use of critical episodes in conjunction with participant narratives, could enable researchers to 'get inside' a task and build richer and more complete descriptions of tasks in action. It is clear that the step we have taken thus far is only a very small one; it is equally clear that now it is necessary to test the applicability of the notion of critical episodes across a wide range of tasks and task types and to examine its role in providing a context for maximizing acquisition potential.

References

BASSANO, S. 1986, Helping learners adapt to unfamiliar methods. *ELT Journal* 40, 13–40.
CARTER, G., LEGUTKE, M. and THOMAS, H. 1987, Experiential learning: Project work in language teaching. Paper presented at the 21st Annual TESOL Convention, Miami.
CROOKES, G. 1986, *Task Classification: A Cross-disciplinary Review*. (Tech. Rep. No. 4) Center for Second Language Classroom Research, Social Science Research Institute, University of Hawai'i.
CROOKES, G. and RULON, K. A. 1985, *Incorporation of Corrective Feedback in Native Speaker/Non-native Speaker Conversation*. (Tech. Rep. No. 3) Center for Second Language Classroom Research, Social Science Research Institute, University of Hawai'i.
HAWKINS, B. 1985, Is an 'appropriate response' always so appropriate? In S. GASS and C. MADDEN (eds) *Input in Second Language Acquisition*. Rowley, MA: Newbury House.
LONG, M. H. 1980, Input, interaction, and second language acquisition. Unpublished PhD dissertation, University of California, Los Angeles.
—— 1985, A role for instruction is second language acquisition: Task based language teaching. In K. HYLTENSTAM and M. PIENEMANN (eds) *Modelling and Assessing Second Language Acquisition*. Clevedon: Multilingual Matters.

ROUNDS, P. L. 1985, Talking the mathematics through: Disciplinary transaction and socio-educational interaction. *Dissertation Abstracts International* 46, 3338A (University Microfilms No. 86-00, 543).
—— 1987, Characterizing successful classroom discourse for NNS teaching assistant training. *TESOL Quarterly* 21, 643–71.
SAMUDA, V. 1990, Task design and the shaping of experience. Paper given at the 24th Annual TESOL Convention, San Francisco.
SWAIN, M. 1985, Communicative competence: Some roles of comprehensible input in its development. In S. GASS and C. MADDEN. *Input in Second Language Acquisition*. Rowley, MA: Newbury House.
TARONE, E. 1988, *Variation in Interlanguage*. London: Edward Arnold.
VARONIS, E. M. and GASS, S. 1985, Non-native/non-native conversations: A model for negotiation of meaning. *Applied Linguistics* 6, 71–90.
YULE, G. and MACDONALD, D. 1990, Resolving referential conflicts in L2 interaction: The effect of proficiency and interactive role. *Language Learning* 40, 539–56.

6 Evaluating Language Learning Tasks in the Classroom

DERMOT F. MURPHY
Thames Valley University, London

Introduction

The proposal that teachers should investigate aspects of what goes on in their classrooms has been with us for some time, and the idea is now being implemented on an increasing scale. One obvious area for consideration in such investigations is that of the language learning tasks used in classrooms. Recently the concept of 'task' has come into focus in various places where writers have begun to explore the concept of task-based learning (TBL) (e.g. Long, 1985; Crookes, 1986; Candlin & Murphy, 1987; Prabhu, 1987; Swales, 1990). Like many basic concepts in applied linguistics and second language pedagogy it is being defined in differing ways. The current scale of attention to evaluation in ESL programs is also relatively recent (e.g. Alderson, 1985; Anivan, 1991; Rea-Dickens & Germaine, 1992), although evaluation studies have a much longer history in the field of education. Evaluation in this sense means more than testing, and has to do with assessing the efficiency and effectiveness of teaching and learning. There has been controversy about how this should be carried out and by whom, particularly whether or not teachers should be involved.

This chapter reports a study of tasks as perceived by a group of young secondary teachers, and looks at the kinds of tasks they selected for use with their classes. The tasks were evaluated by the teachers, with their students, and this dialog about the tasks in use is examined to see how both parties viewed the activities. The influence of the dialog on the teachers' decision-making is also considered. The study does not represent an examination of TBL *per se,* but the issues examined have implications

139

for developing a fuller description of TBL. The questions that were asked in the classroom were concerned with what sorts of things the teacher could learn from the students about the task they had done, and what use the teacher could make of this information. The ability to answer these questions is important if we are to overcome a problem of selection and sequencing in TBL.

The Concept of Task

As a fundamental notion of what we are to discuss, we need to begin with some deliberation of what a task is, and then look at how applied linguists are defining the term with reference to language teaching (I am not concerned here with tasks in experimental research, but see Crookes, 1986). We can then consider what a task-based approach to language learning might be like.

The concept of a task is so everyday as to appear uncontroversial: we all carry out a variety of tasks in our daily lives, at work and at home, and the term refers to a very real concept. However, it seems to be just this breadth and commonplace character of the notion that make precise definition, or agreement on what is meant, difficult to achieve. The idea of purposefulness appears to run through daily tasks, along with connotations of routineness, and repetition; we have to learn to do such tasks, and in most cases how to do them. This would apply from the trivial — brushing your teeth — to the more sophisticated and complex — landing a passenger plane. So tasks also have content, and may be divided either into stages of their execution or into sub-tasks which go to make up the whole; furthermore, the notions of purpose and learning inherent in the concept suggest the possibility of evaluating how well the tasks are executed, or how much progress has been made in acquiring the underlying ability.

In more precise terms, it is not hard to think of a learning task or 'pedagogic task' (Long, 1990) of a purposeful activity carried out in order to acquire some new knowledge or skill, with one set of these learning tasks designed or intended as language learning tasks. Now while many tasks may involve the use of language, uses of language in themselves do not correspond obviously to the order of things we call tasks. Indeed, consideration of activities and their goals may be important for understanding language and language use (Levinson, 1979). In order to teach language, we use specific tasks that are designed to help people learn an L2. We may invent apparently mechanical tasks such as drills, which seem to focus on language for itself, or we may devise apparently communicative tasks such as information-gap exercises, which mimic purposeful activities that involve use of language. In both cases the expectation is that the language will be acquired through carrying out the learning task, where the task acts as a vehicle or catalyst for the learning.

These everyday notions about tasks appear, and seem to be generally agreed on, in definitions of task used in applied linguistics. The purposefulness of tasks is described as 'a specified objective' (Crookes, 1986), and as 'foreseen or emergent goals' (Candlin, 1987). Swales (1990: 75) considers that for designation as a task, an activity must be 'goal-directed'. Long (1985) and Breen (1987) specifically mention content as well as procedures or ways of undertaking the task; and the idea of assessing learner achievement and of evaluation are also mentioned (Long, 1985; Candlin, 1987). The problems begin as we become more specifically concerned with language learning tasks; they are to do with task design and the way that tasks are to be selected and sequenced in programs, though these are not new problems uniquely associated with TBL.

The considerations of task design start from general points such as how well different task-types support the enterprise of language learning, their fit with learner needs, and the learning outcome they are likely to produce. A first question, then, is whether all task types are suitable for use, and Breen (1987: 23) suggests that this is the case, defining tasks as 'workplans . . . from the simple and brief exercise type to more complex and lengthy activities such as group problem-solving or simulations and decision-making'. Swales criticizes this all-encompassing view, suggesting (1990: 74) that the 'simple and brief exercise type' can be seen as an end in itself, which runs contrary to an assumption of the task-based approach, that tasks must enable or support. His argument reflects the view that we can divide language learning activity into mechanical exercises or communicative tasks. The first are associated with the structuralist approach and with marked classroom language usage. This is criticized because it is unlike 'real world' usage, as if classroom usage was somehow unreal, rather than specific because of the situation and activity with which it is associated (see Levinson, 1979; van Lier, 1988). The second category includes tasks such as simulation, information gap, or jigsaw tasks — the kinds of tasks usually referred to in TBL — which enable or support communication.

However, it is difficult to be so categoric. Did structuralists regard the language produced in drills as an end in itself? The answer is 'no'; Lado (1964: 62), for example, wanted simple memorization exercises to give the student language that would have future uses: 'authentic that he [sic] can vary and expand and eventually use in many situations.' This meets Swales' criterion of being calculated to enable or support, and is directed to a long-term goal. The difference now is that we do not expect drills to be sufficient to achieve this goal (though it is worth recalling that some learners did manage this in the bad old structuralist days). By their nature, those in the mechanical category generate imitative, controlled production, but they do not have to be teacher-controlled, and can serve useful learning goals (e.g. Murphy, 1981). Current investigations of tasks in use focused on the communicative category, since these generate varied production, are to a greater or lesser degree in the learners' control, and produce communication-like use of language (e.g. Doughty & Pica, 1986; Pica & Doughty, 1985; for a typology and discussion see Legutke & Thomas, 1991).

However, all this hides the simple point that the classroom function of both categories is to have the learners produce language. At particular stages in learning, controlled, mechanical tasks may help get production going where open-ended tasks requiring ability to negotiate meaning would be too demanding. That does not put the more valuable role of the latter in doubt. These points are sufficient, I hope, to show how difficult it is to argue, in the present state of our knowledge, that there are activities which cannot be admitted to the gallery of language learning tasks.

The influence of specific purpose language teaching (SPLT), with its attention to vocational or occupational needs as determinants of tasks, and the influence of some interpretations of the communicative approach requiring so-called authentic material for tasks (as if this were all that made a task authentic) have led in some quarters to a covert belief in the unreality of the classroom and particularly of what is done there. While we may be conscious of differences between classroom discourse and discourse outside it, we cannot deny the reality of classroom activity, or hope to diminish its specificity. We may seek to vary what is done, but the specificity suggests that there will be classroom tasks, and these require facilitation just as much as the future, external tasks they seek to prepare for. What we need to do is guard against the essentially transactional nature of many classroom tasks, using language to express content, and also create tasks that promote interactional uses of language, to express feelings and interpersonal relations (Brown & Yule, 1983; see also van Lier, 1991).

Implicit in many presentations of tasks is the notion that particular types of task will produce particular types of learning; for example, the reader may be told what sort of questions learners would ask about a picture, but not given a transcript of learners working on the task to support the claim (e.g. Doff, 1988: 210). Although recent research has begun to show that certain types of task influence the language used by the learners involved in the task (for a summary see Crookes, 1986; Ellis, 1990), it does not show the kind of relationship implied, and there is no agreement on what potential may be there for guiding learning (Crookes, 1986: 32). This means that we are still unable to 'apply our knowledge of educational engineering' to produce language learning, as Newmark (1971: 11) pointed out was the case over twenty years ago. The technology for designing tasks according to the criteria we can establish for them is not available: 'at present, the simplicity or complexity of a task, or the variable need to focus on content or form are not easily predictable in advance and perhaps — and perhaps valuably — never will be' (Swales, 1990: 75).

. With notable exceptions, the discussion of tasks is frequently taken from the point of view of the materials designer, or the teacher setting the task for a group of learners, and seems to reflect a common expectation: that the materials and teachers should be in control (e.g. Doff, 1988; Littlewood, 1981). This ignores the learners, their involvement and views — 'our blind spot' (Rudduck, 1991: 30). Learners exercise considerable control over tasks, for, as Breen (1987: 23) points out, 'Learners are capable of playing havoc with even the most carefully designed and much-used task'. He goes on to make a distinction between the task at the design or planning stage, the 'task-as-workplan' and the task as actually accomplished in class or 'task-in-process'. Next he discusses factors such as learners' purposes and attitudes which will redefine the original task for them, and how these new understandings of the task produce a variety of outcomes. Consequently it is not surprising to find that in redefining 'task' Breen (1987: 23) specifically allows for a 'range of outcomes for those who undertake the task'. Two empirical studies show what sort of mismatch arises between teacher intention and learner interpretation. In the first, Wright (1987) shows how learners in a secondary class manipulate the task process, and how the teacher reacts to this as a loss of control. The expected effect of the task is not achieved because the learners control the discourse in order to make the task manageable in their own terms. In the second, Kumaravadivelu (1991) describes ten potential sources of mismatch, producing similar consequences.

It seems important then, to take account of the learner's contribution to task operation, even, as Breen (1987) argues, to involve them in the design of tasks. Candlin (1987) also suggests that in TBL the roles of teacher and learner should be redrawn. They should jointly select the tasks that are to be carried out, so that learners might, for example, choose between different tasks appropriate for their learning objectives, or select alternative routes through the task. This argument for consultation and negotiation, with its consequent reduction in the authority of the teacher, is seen by

Swales (1990: 75) as 'admirable', but he goes on to argue that while they might be a 'valuable concomitant of TBL' they should not be considered a 'necessary condition'. I will argue the opposite case below.

Finally, in this section, we need to consider one of the primary reasons for the current attention to tasks, the proposal that they should form the basis of language learning programs. The main motivation for this interest comes from a dissatisfaction with the different syllabus-types which have guided language teaching over recent decades. Criticism of these is based largely on theoretical argument over the principles and basis of their organization, for example, the notion of simplicity and linguistic elements of most structural syllabuses.

These theoretical objections can also be matched with practical ones. Some teachers ignore, and many do not understand, the curriculum which they reinterpret, before the pupils modify what the teacher offers them! Many teachers rely on the class textbook to direct what is done in class. Woods describes how eight teachers reinterpret a curriculum, focusing on the way two of them make decisions about content and methods:

> (the study) provides an insight into the very individual way in which teachers interpret and reinterpret technical concepts and terms in the light of their everyday teaching experience, leading perhaps to much more complex and textured views than those being imposed from above via language syllabuses and programs. (Woods, 1988: 23–4)

This is a general finding in the field of education (see Sykes (1990: 192) for a more adversely critical account of such reinterpretation and adjustment): 'teachers operate in a system so loosely structured that they will manage and interpret their work over time in ways that minimise stress and difficulty while failing to produce quality education.' The underlying reason given for this reduction in performance is the bargaining that goes on between teacher and student for control. This topic of control is, as we have seen, precisely one of the issues that is raised in discussing TBL, which deserves to be seen in this larger educational context.

In that context the curriculum may be treated as a bureaucratic necessity and is often demonstrably such a monolith, prepared centrally for a whole nation, that fails to take account of very real local differences and factors which the teachers are only too aware of. The different background and attitudes of children in rural schools form one example of local departure from a national norm that may not even represent the majority case. It is not surprising that in these circumstances teachers either consciously reinterpret the directives thay have, or complain that they cannot reconcile what is expected of them with the reality they have to work in. As a consequence the curriculum becomes part of a power struggle in the school that its designers never anticipated.

We do not know enough about language learning to make large-scale, long-terms plans such as national curricula. As previous comments suggest, they usually prove to be idealistic and unwieldy methods of organizing learning, and the change which may come quickly in bureaucratic terms with the introduction of a new curriculum is slow to filter down to the classroom. There, as Swaffar, Arens & Morgan (1982) have shown, teachers are likely to be using a set of universally shared tasks, selected according to their own teaching philosophy rather than ordered according to the priorities established by the curriculum methodology. Various studies have found that tasks form the basis of teachers' lesson planning (see Crookes, 1986; Nunan, 1989), and Woods (1989) shows how short-term teachers' planning is likely to be. An attention to tasks as the basis for learning would, on one level, simply take account of the reality of what teachers do and find operable.

In TBL the tasks themselves become the organizing principle and focus of the learning program. As we have seen above, the traditional elements of the curriculum — goals, content, procedures and evaluation — are taken to be present in tasks. At present all current task-types seem potentially useful to learners, there is no reason to think otherwise. However, their usefulness is determined by their potential to contribute to learning processes and not by their relationship to the content of the curriculum. Focus on content is based on being able to predict learning outcome; focus on process allows that learners will make their own interpretation of tasks. Tasks should be workplans prepared in advance, detailing procedures each learner will work through, rather than the specific outcome the tasks will produce. These proposals offer certain solutions: the task as base unit attempts to solve the problem with the unwieldiness and insensitivity of the curriculum, while the task as procedure attempts to cope with the learners' control of task outcome and relevance. There remains the problem of finding a route for learners. This point will be picked up at the end of the next section.

Evaluation in the Classroom

The idea of teachers conducting investigations into what is happening in their classrooms, like many of the ideas about tasks, has been around for some time, but has come into greater prominence as educators realize that change has to take place in the school through teachers (see Rudduck, 1991; Sykes, 1990). However, this requires teachers to undertake a new role, and

the term 'teacher as researcher' (Stenhouse, 1975), still causes some awk-
wardness (see examples in Murphy, 1985; Cherchali-Fadel, 1990). However, teachers are increasingly undertaking this role, whether as 'teacher–
researcher', 'reflective practitioner', or 'enquiring teacher'. Whatever the
title used, such teachers are involved in the investigation of practical issues
or problems in their classrooms, in carrying out evaluation to get information that may help to identify a solution or provide understanding of what is
happening. The findings may not be of immediate use, but that is a risk of
any investigation.

Evaluation is concerned with assessing the efficiency and effectiveness
of teaching and learning; it may be summative, that is, it may account for
how far the program has reached its objectives, or formative, that is it may
be carried out as a trouble-shooting operation to help make practical, but
justified changes or adjustments in the operation of a learning program. The
goals of the evaluation may be to assess cost effectiveness, or to check on
performance; they may be to develop the program; or they may be concerned with providing a means for professional development of teachers
(e.g. Hopkins, 1985).

Evaluation may then be designed to help teachers with their management of the programme. Nunan (1989: 7) describes how a consultant was
able to help an experienced teacher having difficulty operating a negotiated
curriculum with a particular class. Through discussions which evaluated the
situation the teacher arrived at a way to approach the problems, and successfully solved them through evaluative discussion with the students. Even
where the curriculum is centrally planned it is possible to involve teachers in
evaluation to face up to, investigate, or even solve the problems that are
within their control (Murphy, 1991).

This is a cue to go back to our discussion of TBL. We had reached a
point of suggesting that a task-based approach would not have a planned
curriculum, but a resource or set of tasks available to the teacher and learners. However, as various writers have pointed out, at this stage problems
of selection, sequencing and grading remain (e.g. Long, 1985; Candlin,
1987). How do teacher and learner decide which task to proceed to next?
What do teacher and learner identify as a task? How does the teacher know
whether a task suited the learner, that is to say, interested them and was, in
their view, controllable?

The problem described is a managerial one that, I propose, could be
solved through a process of formative evaluation. Teacher and learners will
need a constant dialog of the kind just described in the example from Nunan
and, contrary to Swales' opinion cited earlier, if the teacher is to guide the

learners and take account of their element of control, as well as their insight into their learning, then this process must involve both parties. As the example shows, the proposal and way of proceeding are in fact independent of a task-based approach. Any approach might benefit from such consultation, while individual teachers would be empowered to undertake their own professional development. Its significance for TBL is considerable, though, because it offers a solution to a fundamental problem of the approach. The study which is described next represents an attempt to explore this proposal, though not within the context of a task-based approach.

The Study

The subjects of the study

The evaluation was carried out by twenty teachers working in secondary schools in rural and urban areas on the East Coast of peninsular Malaysia. The work was carried out in two phases, in 1989 and 1990, with eight teachers in the first group and twelve in the second; the two groups had no contact over the investigation or its findings. The teachers volunteered to take part, and in fact six more volunteered but did not complete any of the evaluations; all were Malaysian and non-native speakers. In each case there were six weeks available for the evaluation.

The teachers were following a centrally specified curriculum; they were teaching mainly Moslem pupils, the majority of whom came from farming and fishing families. Each teacher selected one of their classes for the study; 19 of them worked with fourth-year classes (students aged between 15 and 16), and one worked with a fifth-year class. The class size ranged from 15 to 42, with an average size of just over 27 students; the classes, with one exception, were co-educational.

The teachers were told that the evaluation they were to carry out had as its aims:

1. to find out pupil reaction to particular tasks in terms of interest and usefulness; and
2. to use this information in selecting tasks and guiding their pupils.

They were asked to record the information for analysis and study later. They had no formal training in evaluation before the study. After two initial meetings, to set up and explain the study, they met again as a group on two occasions, and I saw them all individually in their schools so that it was possible to discuss progress and difficulties.

The study method

There were various steps in the study. At the completion of a task the teachers were asked to distribute the questionnaire in Figure 1 to the students. The top version is shown as it was presented, in the pupils' mother tongue (Bahasa Malaysia); the bottom version is the English translation. In use 'task' was usually taken to refer to lesson or period.

Kelas ....   Tarikh ....

Bulatkan jawapan anda. Adakah latihan ini:

1 MENYERONAKKAN // MEMBOSANKAN ?

2 BERGUNA UNTUK SAYA // TIDAK BERGUNA

Terimah kasi!

Class ....   Date ....

Circle your answers. Was this task:

1 FUN // BORING ?   2 NO USE // GOOD FOR ME?

Thank you!

FIGURE 1   *Questionnaire handed to pupils on completion of a task*

The teachers were free to decide when they would use the questionnaire, but it was recommended that they use them twice a week. When they first used the questionnaire, they explained the purpose to the class in terms of the aims they had been given. The parameters chosen for the questionnaire, and by implication for the teacher–learner discussion are 'interest' and 'usefulness'. These notions are discussed further below. Interest is glossed in the questionnaire as 'fun', and the teachers were told to explain to the class that this also meant 'challenging, interesting, relevant, enjoyable', or the reverse — 'boring'. Usefulness is glossed as 'good for you', to be explained as 'helps you to learn something, to understand something, to make something easier for you', or 'not good for me', that is 'unhelpful, difficult, unclear'. The terms in the questionnaire were discussed with some of the teachers, who provided the translation.

Some teachers found it was useful to encourage the learners to write comments on the questionnaire slips. There was general agreement that the questionnaire results were not accurate as students were usually reluctant, despite anonymity, to comment adversely; discussion with the class showed, for example, that while only three students had circled 'boring', several would later volunteer to say why the task was boring. In the end, the questionnaire became a way of focusing attention and a prompt for the next stage. After the class the teachers then took the questionnaires away to analyze them.

At the beginning of the following lesson the teachers were to ask the class why people had said the task was, for example, 'fun but no use'; however, experience showed that it was easier to deal with one term at a time. The discussion was slow to start as the students were reluctant to comment; however, by asking, 'If someone said that yesterday's task was boring, why would they have done that?', previously silent students began to join the discussion, speaking on others' behalf! After the class the teachers recorded the discussion in a diary, where they also noted details of the task, the questionnaire results and any comments of their own. They agreed that the diaries would be available to me, and that I could copy and quote from them anonymously.

There were, then, four steps to the evaluation:

1. completion of the questionnaire after the task;
2. analysis of the replies;
3. discussion of the replies with the class;
4. recording the discussion in a diary.

Taking the four steps as one cycle, we get the picture of the study as shown in Table 1. As these figures suggest, most of the group did not complete the expected number of cycles, and several teachers dropped out of the study after two weeks. They completed between two and eight cycles each (range).

TABLE 1

	Teachers	Period	Cycles	Range	Average
Group 1	8	2–6 weeks	46	3–8	5.75
Group 2	12	2–5 weeks	53	2–6	4.40
Total	20		99		4.95

Two and a half to three months after the research period, I interviewed 19 of the 20 teachers about the experience of conducting the evaluation and what they felt it had achieved. The data from the diaries and the interviews form the basis for the study. Both diary and interview data are cited anonymously in the sections which follow, but the first letter in brackets is a randomly assigned identity to show which teacher recorded or made this comment; the second letter shows whether the information comes from a diary entry (D) or from an interview (I); where the data recorded are written comments from a pupil. These are put in quotation marks.

The design of the investigation was based on a need to achieve a systematic, non-threatening way for the teacher to open a dialog with the learners. The idea for the questionnaire and discussion came from Allwright (personal communication), and the diary was to provide a record for both teacher and researcher. Diary entries are often criticized as research data for being selective and self-flattering, and while there is evidence for this (but then which teachers are not pleased to find that the class likes them and what they do together?), there are also records of failure, and of student dissatisfaction. The selective nature of the data cannot be overlooked though, as teachers did not choose tasks at random for evaluation, and some describe their selectiveness: ' I didn't want to do it with certain tasks; either there was no time or I find the task difficult, boring, not interesting.' (BI)

The interview data are also subject to particular scrutiny in this study as I was well known to the subjects both as tutor and supervisor in their training, where we had had prolonged contact over some time. I can only claim that by the time the interviews were conducted the teachers knew that I expected them to be frank with me, and to talk about adverse as well as favorable aspects of what had been done. Certainly those who had dropped out of the study were not afraid to tell me why. The study was proposed, and I believe conducted, as a cooperative enterprise and was independent of any assessment of the teacher's work.

This study falls within a tradition of ethnographic investigation, and the findings reported next are based on an analysis of the sets of data to identify common themes and salient entries. The data were re-analyzed later to cross-check findings.

The classroom data

This section is concerned with answers to the first question:

1. How much information can teachers find out from their learners about the tasks they use?

The diary entries in fact cover far more than this, and their scope includes aspects of lesson aims, content, materials, management, and learning as well as any verbatim comments from learners. There are also comments on the research procedure, and indications of the effects the information had on teachers' actions, which is dealt with in the next section.

The findings reported here are grouped according to focus, and include sample positive and negative comments. Often categories will overlap, but the example is chosen to illustrate the theme. Comments which do not relate to tasks are included to show the range of learner views and what they considered important. The teachers' agenda was to discuss tasks, the learners changed this task and their replies are significant, as will become clear in discussion.

Task aims

Where these are recorded they differ from the teacher's or expand on the teacher's stated aim. Where this was to 'construct dialogues according to (language) function given', the discussion revealed that

> Pupils' aims for yesterday's task: to get knowledge, to learn to speak/ use English in 'real' life, important for the tests and exams, useful for the future — being able to speak and write English. (TD)

On another occasion the same teacher found the learners had other aims:

> A number of pupils had actually asked me the pronunciation of certain words even though it was not my intention to focus on pronunciation. (TD)

Sometimes the teacher's aim is not recognized, and the task is dismissed as purposeless:

> They enjoyed the lesson but still they do not know the purpose of it: they regard the activity as having no connection with their education. (AD)

> It was not useful as it is not in the syllabus. (ZD)

Task content

Real-life usefulness, or help with accuracy appear as valuable content:

> Making telegrams is interesting and very useful, what is more interesting — their telegram is being used by others to make a conversation using it — the ideal of 'audience'. (HD)

> It was easy to understand and gave them some useful tips to use the prepositions. (UD)

The learners reject tasks where some aspect of the content is considered too difficult:

> The task help them to improve their reading but because they didn't really know the right pronunciation they became rather confused and bored. (DD)

The teacher encounters a similar difficulty in another lesson:

> The task was boring and not useful because they did not understand some of the words in the passage. (DD)

Materials and task

There are several comments that relate to the teacher's materials, the creativity that has gone into them, and how helpful they are for learning:

> 'Today I understand the lesson because there is some objects to help me understand what I do better.' (YD)

The textbook is not popular:

> They liked it when I brought in materials from the outside — magazines, pictures and brochures — and didn't use the textbook. (GI)

> They also mention about not being depended on textbooks which sometimes can be very boring! (CD)

The learners are demanding about standards:

> 'About the soul singer. I think teacher should find a poster or picture of a singer or a actor not to draw it. It's look ugly.' (HD)

> 'I think you should take some handsome guys for our suspect so we look forward to investigate them.' (HD)

Where the learners are given choice and an element of control over the task, the reaction is positive:

> All said it was interesting and fun; like it because they were given the opportunity (for the first time) to choose their own tasks and not the teacher who prepared everything for them. By doing this they knew what they could do or manage to do according to their own ability and level; they also like the idea of presenting the task to everybody in the class. Tasks included 'how to make a birthday card', 'how to make a book marker'. (CD)

Management

Requests for variety appear frequently and concern many aspects of what is done:

I had used a variety of techniques in one lesson, so they didn't feel bored. (GI)

They expect me to do different sorts of things, not to repeat things, not something similar. (KI)

The teachers were introducing the use of groupwork in these schools and reflections on this come up frequently:

They liked learning in groups: they could exchange information, friends could explain, it taught them to work together, the works somehow became easier for them to do; when I learned that, I did groupwork in almost every lesson. (GI)

However, colleagues were not so enthusiastic:

Teachers don't agree with my style of teaching. They don't like group-work. (QD)

There are several lessons for the teachers to learn about their handling of the class:

I think I underestimated my PP; I wasn't patient enough to wait a minute for a person to stand up, think and utter the answer. (HD)

I had to keep them busy, they didn't like to be kept waiting. (ND)

One thing was my way of giving instructions: they said I do it so fast and all in English they wanted me to speak slowly and use different sentences and words. (FI) (also in FD)

Learning

The language used for instruction is important, but there is not agreement on this:

They like it when I used more English and less mother tongue. (YI)

Some do need translation, they think that if they don't know all the words they are not satisfied, they won't accept just getting the gist. (SI)

Pupils want me to explain again in mother tongue. (TD)

Newness and variety combined with active involvement are seen positively, and their absence noted:

They said it's a new activity so it was interesting, they hate the old boring style of teaching where they are not involved in the activity. (HD)

They expect me to do different sorts of things, not to repeat things, not something similar. (KI)

The learner's politeness and respect may risk masking a problem:

'I know this lesson is very useful to me and the others but I don't understand.' (YD)

One teacher reports an interesting example of pupils recognizing that some of their peers may help them:

In groupwork I mixed boys and girls, then they separated themselves; they didn't like mixed groups because no one had done it in school before, I don't think they'd even used groupwork. But the boys who went to the girls' groups were the weaker ones: they knew the girls would give them better help. The good girls are more tolerant, the good boys just wanted to express their own ideas and not to help the weak ones. (AI)

Atmosphere

A number of entries show that, in the words of one teacher who was particularly sensitive to atmosphere:

Moods and feelings really play an important part in learning activity. (HD)

We laughed and had fun today — I didn't know they were so clever in making things up. (HD)

She picked up both positive and negative aspects; her colleagues focus on negative aspects:

The lesson was boring because I did not smile at all. (FD)

Not enjoyable because it was in the afternoon and they felt sleepy and tired. (DD)

There was no understanding between each member of the group, therefore they were less interested to do the activity. There was quite a hostile environment. (AD)

Teacher

Several of the written comments are addressed personally to the teacher:

Some of them wrote 'good teacher' or 'best teacher' 'The best English teacher' 'we trust you' 'remember us' on their slips. (DD)

'Each day T gets more interesting not only in terms of teaching but in physical appearance as well.' (SD)

Teachers as evaluators

This section examines the replies and comments relevant to the second question, concerning the information just dealt with:

2. What effect will this information have on classroom management and planning?

The data here cover comments on the research procedure and indications of the effects the information had on the teachers' action.

Dialog and control

The data here concern the teachers' reactions to doing the evaluation. An open dialog between teachers and learners about what they are doing together is generally perceived as threatening teacher control of the class, and more than half of the teachers recalled their anxiety about surrendering part of their authority:

I was a bit anxious to start. (YI)

In a way I felt it was threatening. (HI)

I felt not too happy. (GI)

I felt awkward at first. (RI)

Others had more favorable memories of starting the evaluation:

I was intrigued. (QI)

I felt enthusiastic at first. (JI)

The evaluation procedure was appreciated for the focus it gave to the teachers' work, for what it revealed about the pupils, and for the different relationship it created. The first cycle prompted this reaction from one teacher:

It made me more aware of my own teaching — makes me wonder: 'Did I teach too fast?' 'Did my students learn?' (BD)

Several mention the fact that this was extra work, a chore, but found some rewards:

It's hard work but it's interesting; I feel it was threatening but it was interesting. I got a letter from them; they said it was nice to do this because they did not feel threatened by me, to know that you are their friend and they can confide in you. (HI)

Another teacher learned to include this in her routine, and, moreover, was aware of the benefits she was gaining, even from the learners' negative comments:

It wasn't really a lot of work; I could fit it in with other things. Sometimes their comments may hurt but it's best to rectify rather than leave it until you can't do anything about it. (SI)

For others the procedure was not revealing, or they found that the pupils resisted the proffered dialog:

Sometimes they asked me again why do you have to do this, so I explained it again. They find it curious, or said no not this again. They hate the idea of thinking back about the lesson and having to say something about it. (KI)

I didn't feel too happy; I stopped doing this because the PP found it boring: I kept asking them the same questions, they didn't really want to write down the answers, they were bored and didn't want to do it again. (GI)

Effects on planning

As might be expected, given the variety of pupil comment and suggestion, the effects of the dialog in terms of the influence on the teachers were varied and do not appear to follow any pattern; too few of them did enough. Much of the data on this came out in the interviews, so are prompted and benefit from hindsight. The things mentioned include:

Confidence:

The most useful thing was how it made me feel. The way the pupils' comments can have an effect on my confidence as a teacher: whenever they say something like it's boring, it makes me feel sad, disappointed; but if they say it helps then I feel good. (SI)

Content, method, and task design

You think more about it — what you need to teach, methods to use. It made me think again about the shape of the activity; writing it up I thought I mustn't do it like that again or I must do that, it caught their interest. (HI)

They said what sort of things they wanted me to teach and the way they wanted me to teach. (ZI)

The change was not necessarily made with the subject class:

If I used the same task with a different class I revised my plan. (CI)

One teacher did regularly note ideas about changes to make on the basis of the class discussion, and these range over points of content:

do not teach the terms 'pronoun', 'noun', 'verb' in isolation,

to points of management:

avoid demotivating task: some students were afraid to act out the dialogue; therefore must be careful when nominating student. (JD)

Management: Other comments relating to management include one supported in both sets of data:

I became more relaxed about timing, about allowing them to finish rather than me finish my lesson plan, allowing them to get the most out of things. (YI and YD)

Planning and selecting the tasks: One teacher felt that the learners' comments, which are also recorded in the diary influenced lesson planning:

Doing this had an effect; I didn't think that my lesson was so systematic but when they said that I paid attention to get each step connected one to another, I kept their ideas in mind when choosing activities. (SI)

Most of the group, however, sum up positive experience in less precise terms:

I was able in the end to help them better. (AI)

For others the outcome was not so positive, and one diary entry, for example, shows that the feedback from the learners was not used:

I didn't revise my plans according to this information. (ND)

Implications for TBL

In this final section I want to review the findings from the data to see how far they support the proposal made above: in order to overcome the problem of selecting and sequencing tasks in a task-based approach, teachers will need to evaluate tasks-in-process with the learners. To make this assessment we need to consider four criteria:

1. Can teachers carry out this evaluation on a frequent basis?
2. Does the evaluation provide information relevant to selection of tasks?
3. Does the evaluation provide information relevant to sequencing of tasks?
4. Will learners participate in the evaluation?

Operability

For these teachers the evaluation was not crucial to operation of the approach they were using; they also encountered problems with the learners, which will be discussed later, but which in many cases proved a major factor in dropping the study. All we are interested in at this stage is assessing whether or not teachers can take on the additional job of carrying out evaluation, whether they can interpret and use the findings they obtain, and what effect this has on their role as teacher. Although some did not succeed, or found it difficult to carry out the evaluation, enough did manage to include this extra task without wasting time. The interpretation and use of findings is not as convincing as the proposals would require, but then the group had no particular training in carrying out evaluation, so these results simply suggest a need for training in this area. The effect of the dialog with the learners does represent a change in their relationship, but where the teacher carried on with evaluation, this change was seen very positively.

Information for selecting tasks

As we have seen, the findings include a lot of information beyond that which was looked for. In effect the evaluation allowed the teachers to gauge what Allwright & Bailey (1991: 158) have called receptivity, and define as openness, contrasted with defensiveness on the part of the learners. The replies show an awareness and concern for the whole of their learning, and emphasize how the task is embedded in a social encounter. The data certainly show information, which even if it was not always heeded, could be used by the teacher to select tasks, according to difficulty, perceived relevance, stimulation, helpfulness and learner contribution among other points.

Information for sequencing tasks

Only one teacher indicates that the information from the learners influenced the planning of steps in activities. In that case it is clear as well that the steps are within the activity, rather than indicating what steps are made from one task to another. The information may not be there because the learners were not being asked for it, and when they do request a task it is for more of the same after carrying out an unfamiliar or new task such as listening comprehension based on a pop song. There is, then, no evidence to support this aspect of the proposal, but equally there is no evidence to suggest that it could not be achieved.

Learner participation

The results suggest that teachers can find out a range of information from their learners, which both seem to find helpful. This depends on both sides finding the procedure positive and perceiving it as beneficial:

[The research was] useful, particularly the relationship between me and the pupils; they liked it because no one had done that with them. They weren't threatened, they became frank. They thought it a good idea the teacher should talk to them. (YI)

For those members of the group who did not have a positive experience of using the procedure, the discouraging effect of their pupils' resistance to the change the teachers were introducing, confirms other researchers' experience of involving secondary pupils in such research:

When pupils *are* taken inside the walls of the teacher's mind and given access to the logic that sequences their learning tasks, they are not much bothered to exercise their right to know and understand. (Rudduck, 1991: 54, her emphasis)

It also confirms another of Rudduck's remarks about the learners' role in innovation:

we underestimate the force for conservatism that pupils can represent. (Rudduck, 1991: 30)

Any attempt to introduce TBL, or to set up classroom evaluation of this kind, will need to take the learners and their beliefs and feelings fully into account.

I want to conclude with some questions which I feel need to be answered before these proposals can be taken further. The teachers had no background in classroom research, and no specific training for carrying out evaluation before the preparatory sessions of this study. In the interviews, some of the teachers commented that having read about evaluation and classroom research in the interval between the research and the interview, they could understand the research aims better. This raises the question:

1. What effect would better preparation of the teachers have on conducting research like this?

It is tempting to preempt the answer.

One thing pupils want from their teachers is conformity. Some of these pupils showed resistance to innovative behavior on the part of one of their teachers, and this hostility to straying from their classroom agenda raises the further question:

2. Would better briefing of the learners increase acceptance of the dialog? The time available for the research was relatively brief and it would be interesting to have an answer to this question:

3. What effect would longer term use have with better briefed users? The most desirable scenario would be, of course, to conduct the research within a TBL program.

Acknowledgements

With their permission, I particularly want to thank Adilah, Ashikin, Aspalila, Azlin, Azman, Juliana, Latifah, Mimi, Mina, Norhafizah, Norzakiah, Nurafida, Parames, Rafidah, Rohana, Sarima, Siti Samira, Suzana, Yang, and Zurina; they did all the hard work.

References

ALDERSON, J. C. (ed.) 1985, *EVALUATION*, Lancaster Practical Papers in English Language Education, vol. 6. Oxford: Pergamon Press.

ALLWRIGHT, D. and BAILEY, K. 1991, *Focus on the Language Classroom*. Cambridge: Cambridge University Press.

ANIVAN, S. (ed.) 1991, *Issues in Language Programme Evaluation in the 1990's*. Singapore: RELC.

BREEN, M. P. 1987, Learner contributions to task design. In C. N. CANDLIN and D. F. MURPHY (eds). *Language Learning Tasks*. Englewood Cliffs, NJ: Prentice Hall International.

BROWN, G. and YULE, G. 1983, *Discourse Analysis*. Cambridge: Cambridge University Press.

CANDLIN, C. N. 1987, Towards task-based language learning. In C. N. CANDLIN and D. F. MURPHY (eds) *Language Learning Tasks*. Englewood Cliffs, NJ: Prentice Hall International.

CHERCHALI-FADEL, S. 1990, The notion of learner-centredness: How it worked out in the literature? In M. OUAKRIM and A. ZAKI (eds) *English Language Teaching: The Maghrebi Experience*. Agadir Fes: Moroccan Association of Teachers of English.

CROOKES, G. 1986, *Task Classification: A Cross-disciplinary Review*. (Tech. Rep. No. 4). Center for Second Language Classroom Research, Social Science Research Insitute, University of Hawaii.

DOFF, A. 1988, *Teach English: A Training Course for Teachers* (Trainer's Handbook). Cambridge: Cambridge University Press.

DOUGHTY, C. and PICA, T. 1986, 'Information gap' tasks: Do they facilitate second language acquisition? *TESOL Quarterly* 20, 305–25.

ELLIS, R. 1990, *Instructed Second Language Acquisition*. Oxford: Basil Blackwell.

HOPKINS, D. 1985, *A Teachers' Guide to Classroom Research*. Milton Keynes: Open University Press.

KUMARAVADIVELU, B. 1991, Language learning tasks: Teacher intention and learner interpretation. *ELT Journal* 45, 98–107.

LADO, R. 1964, *Language Teaching: A Scientific Approach*. New York: McGraw Hill.

LEGUTKE, M. and THOMAS, H. 1991, *Process and Experience in the Classroom*. New York: Longman.
LEVINSON, S. C. 1979, Activity types and language. *Linguistics* 17, 5/6, 365–99.
LITTLEWOOD, W. 1981, *Communicative Language Teaching: An Introduction*. Cambridge: Cambridge University Press.
LONG, M. 1985, A role for instruction in second language acquisition: Task-based language training. In K. HYLTENSTAM and M. PIENEMANN (eds) *Modelling and Assessing Second Language Acquisition*. Clevedon: Multilingual Matters.
—— 1990, Task, group and task-group interactions. In S. ANIVAN (ed.) *Language Teaching Methodology for the Nineties*. Singapore: RELC.
MURPHY, D. F. 1981, Living without a lab. *Practical English Teaching* 2, 24–5.
—— 1985, Evaluation in language teaching: Assessment, accountability and awareness. In J. C. ALDERSON (ed.) *Evaluation* (pp. 1–17). Lancaster Practical Papers in English Language Education, vol. 6. Oxford: Pergamon Press.
—— 1991, Principles and practice in an evaluation project. In S. ANIVAN (ed.) *Issues in Language Programme Evaluation in the 1990's* (pp. 26–34). Singapore: RELC.
NEWMARK, L. 1971, A minimal language teaching program. In P. PIMSLEUR and T. QUINN (eds) *The Psychology of Second Language Learning*. Cambridge: Cambridge University Press.
NUNAN, D. 1989, *Understanding Language Classrooms*. New York: Prentice Hall.
PICA, T. and DOUGHTY, C. 1985, Input and interaction in the communicative language classroom: A comparison of teacher-fronted and group activities. In S. GASS and C. MADDEN (eds) *Input and Second Language Acquisition*. Rowley, MA: Newbury House.
PRABHU, N. S. 1987, *Second Language Pedagogy*. Oxford: Oxford University Press.
REA-DICKENS, P. and GERMAINE, K. 1992, *Evaluation*. Oxford: Oxford University Press.
RUDDUCK, J. 1991, *Innovation and Change*. Milton Keynes: Open University Press.
STENHOUSE, L. 1975, *An Introduction to Curriculum Research and Development*. London: Heinemann.
SWAFFAR, J. K., ARENS, K. and MORGAN, M. 1982, Teacher practices: Redefining method as task hierarchy. *Modern Language Journal* 66, 24–33.
SWALES, J. M. 1990, *Genre Analysis*. Cambridge: Cambridge University Press.
SYKES, G. 1990, Evaluation in the context of national policy and local organization. In M. GRANHEIM, M. KOGAN and U. P. LUNDGREN (eds) *Evaluation as Policy Making*. London: Jessica Kingsley Publishers.
VAN LIER, L. 1988, *The Classroom and the Language Learner*. New York: Longman.
—— 1991, Inside the classroom: Learning process and teaching procedures. *Applied Language Learning* 2, 29–69.
WOODS, D. 1988, Teachers' interpretation of second language teaching curricula. Centre for Applied Language Studies, Carleton University, Ottawa.
—— 1989, Studying ESL teachers' decision-making: Rationale, methodological issues, and initial results. *Carleton Papers in Applied Language Studies* 6, 107–23.
WRIGHT, T. 1987, Instructional task and discoursal outcome in the L2 classroom. In C. N. CANDLIN and D. F. MURPHY (eds) *Language Learning Tasks*. Englewood Cliffs, NJ: Prentice Hall International.

Index